AMERICAN WOMEN
Our Spirituality in Our Own Words

AMERICAN WOMEN
Our Spirituality in Our Own Words

Catherine Racette
Peg Reynolds, C.S.J.

TM

Bear & Company
Santa Fe, New Mexico

Bear & Company Books are published by Bear &
Company, Inc. Its Trademark, consisting of the
words "Bear & Company" and the portrayal of the
bear, is Registered in the U.S. Patent and Trademark Office and in other countries Marca Regis-
trada Bear & Company, Inc., P.O. Drawer 2860
Santa Fe, NM 87504

Typesetting—Casa Sin Nombre, Santa Fe, NM
Cover Design—William Field
Printed in the United States by BookCrafters, Inc.

To Peggy

Table of Contents

Chapter Three: Living Simply

Chapter Five: Being Oppressed

Preface and Acknowledgment

I like to begin at the end. The Abbey at Snowmass, Colorado, was a perfect setting to begin reflecting, re-capturing the experience of the 9-week journey of being with women throughout the country; playing in their environment; praying and breaking bread at their tables; sleeping in their waterbeds or on a hardwood floor next to the blessed sacrament; bathing in their warm water; exchanging lives and ideas of lives to come. How did this all come about? It was not easy. In fact, it was extremely difficult as we met obstacle upon obstacle from the inception of the dream. We owe a heartfelt thanks to hundreds of women and men who supported this vision for their selfless hospitality and receptivity.

The dream that became a reality began on a walk in the woods one day in the winter of '78 as words were exchanged and the dialogue gave birth to the idea. No idea is born except in pain. No idea is carried out but in pain. No idea is completed but in pain. The pain and the pleasure of this project continue to this day (spring of '84). The Abbey was the perfect place to recollect, recall, remember what had evolved throughout the journey.

The intent was not to interpret their lives, but to ask in compassion, what they were going through. In order to do this, I had to ask myself what I had gone through as a woman. I had to ask myself why I had been denied certain truths; why ! was experiencing a fear of failure and lack of confidence. I had to ask why women have been known to suffer more and why we have been buried by suffering and honored and praised for suffering. I, as a woman, had to ask myself why children are rejected at birth, why men are despised, why women are screaming a war cry with the earth rebelling at rape. I, as a woman, have grown in asking, have groaned in growth in asking why I cannot be loved by another woman.

I, as woman, had to ask why man cannot be friend when the love affair is over. I, as a woman, so totally aware of our feminine weakness, our uncertainty, envy, jealousy, compulsive desire for love and dependency, always finding a place to put the blame. I, as a woman, who grew up in a society that denied me the right to know the truth about my body; who grew through adolescence unaware of the most beautiful natural processes within, now moving through adulthood struggling to uneducate myself and constantly having to defend a celibate position.

In all this, though, what motivated me was the knowledge of my passion for people and my gift for love. And so, in the mountains of the Abbey, I found myself frightfully grateful for the blessing of having this opportunity to go into the lives of these common women to sensitively move them to encounter connections within their experiences and carry them out of their experiences—many times untouched moments, many times hidden pains, many times cries in the unending wilderness.

I was grateful and am grateful still for the honor, the privilege of probing the hearts of these women. This is why I committed myself to the vision. I have lived my life as a woman, cried with it, embraced it, have been playfully grateful for the creation of it. Because of this, it has eased the pain of asking these women what they have gone through. These women have asked us to give to you their stories, not to judge or compare, but to "see" how they have survived, come back, been brought back alive, unscarred, no final wounds even.

I wish to thank the Sisters of St. Joseph of LaGrange, Illinois, for taking the risk, and all the people I've lived with since 1978 (including myself) for supporting my questionable existence; the House of Promise; John and Judy Calix; Pam Montagno; the Dennises; Mary Dunn; and Jolene and Joshua Vance. A special thanks to my friend Bill Lupo; my sister Elizabeth Rusin; Darlene and Rick Adam; and Maureen and Michael Fahey. I am grateful too for all my teachers, wherever they are, especially Brian Swimme, a physicist who believes the unbelievable and pushes and prods.

Finally, I thank an unnamed psychologist who said I was not mad, but rather co-operating with the mysterious. (He was advised by a theologian.) And, of course, Bear & Company, the publishers of creation-centered spirituality!

Catherine Racette
Lone Tree, Iowa
April, 1984

CHAPTER ONE:
DYING AND RISING

"We don't know what the resurrection is. We simply know it is a transformation. If you believe that, it should take the edge off. You are going to experience it in a context that isn't final. It is a question of belief rather than reason, and everything I know about life now teaches me that reason is very small and perhaps one of the least trustworthy things of life.

"I've been through a number of deaths and resurrections. When someone survives, I don't always know who it is." That's what it is . . . an identity crisis."

——Marge Hughes, West Virginia

SUSAN JEANSONNE "I found God out of despair, I guess."

JO DORR "How do we age gracefully? Creatively?"

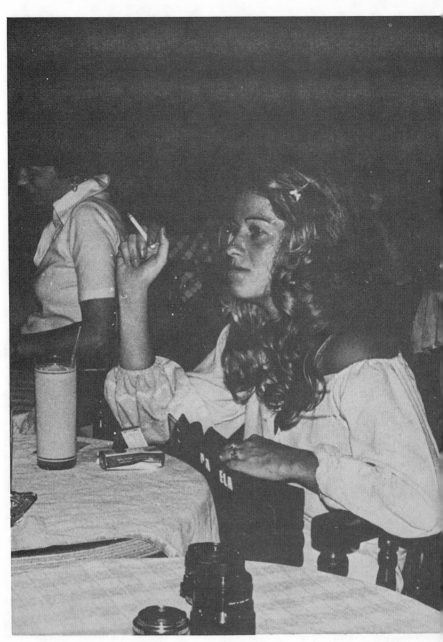

PAMELA ST. DENIS "I cannot afford to lose anything that I love or trust right now."

MARGE HUGHES "Death is like rebirth."

IRENE MARIE LOWLEY "Most of the time I occupied myself with my duties toward my children and my home."

SUSAN JEANSONNE *(Littleton, Massachusetts.) Coordinator of The Beginning Experience: a national movement for divorced, separated, or widowed. Age: 41. Education: High school.*

Battered wife, divorced, remarried; blended family of five children.

Excerpt from Journal:
The evening was going to be bad. The signs were clear to me. The drinking had started about an hour before. The tension and feeling of controlled violence were building. I was relieved when I was able to get the children all to bed without their realizing what was happening. Laura had an indication and perhaps the boys, but they had learned to keep quiet. Laura, living on the edge of desperation, always tried to ask me about things. As I put her to bed, all she had time for was a hurried, "Do you think it's going to be bad?" I tried to reassure her, but her father came in and so the goodnights ended.

Knowing there was nothing I could do to change his course, I decided that I would go to bed, and just maybe he would let me be, and then there would be no recipient for his anger. That was not to be. I had been in bed reading for about five minutes when he came in, bringing his bottle of vodka. After slamming the book out of my hand and standing over me, he gradually started talking about how terribly I had treated him, what a good person he was, how I shouldn't be allowed to get away with how I acted.

I had had a knot in my stomach all evening, and now my whole body was having waves of weakness and warmth and chills go through it. I tried to stay calm and not add to or fan his anger. He just kept right on building it. He talked about the fact that if I couldn't live with him I shouldn't live at all and that he had decided he might as well kill me.

He went to the closet and took out his pistol. He came over, sat down, and put the gun to my temple. The coldness of the metal was a shock and almost a relief. Now I knew where things had been heading. No more being scared by wondering. He continued to talk as he pulled back the hammer and I heard the click. I accepted the fact that I would die very soon. I thought of the children but knew that there was nothing I could do for them. I had been removed from any active part of life other than to cause the last explosion. I thought of my relatives, but nothing seemed that important.

When I faced the reality of my death and accepted it, there was a beautiful sense of peace and calm—real calm and detached joy that flowed through me. Gone were the knot in the stomach, the warm and cold waves, and flashes; in their place an all-over feeling of all-encompassing peace, with myself and with others. I had no feeling toward Virgil—he was outside of my world—no worry about the children. I was somewhere beyond that, removed from that world. I thought of God, and I associated my good feelings with Him. I was sure that I would finally reach the closeness and understanding that I had strived for here on earth. I knew His love was waiting for me, and I was not afraid.

This feeling stayed with me for quite a while. Then I gradually felt that I was coming back to being a participant in my life again. I was aware that Virgil was still drinking and still talking, but there was a difference. His mood was changing. He was talking about the men he had killed, and he got up to get his knife so that he could field dress me if he wanted to after he killed me. He told me how you do this. But it was as though I could see his mood dissipating. Death was not present that minute but was receding to minutes away. I didn't know if it would return that close again, but I knew that it was possible. I also knew that for some reason I did not die when I had been going to.

The gun was held to my head, cocked, for one and a half hours. I had no awareness of time. After the first few minutes there was just a floating sensation. Coming back into this world was sad, it meant I was not finished. The peace had felt so good. But I wasn't depressed. It was just a matter-of-fact reality. I must continue. I must figure out what to do, depending on what happened moment to moment. But I knew I was different. I knew that to have survived after being on the point of death in such a manner for such a length of time meant that God was not ready for me to quit. I knew that there must be some purpose in my living, but I didn't know what.

A lot of people are searching for something they don't have a name for. A lot of people start out with the advantage of being sensitive to their own feelings, and others come by it in different ways. But once they start getting in touch with their feelings and really try to understand themselves and other people, I think that's a part of becoming a whole human being, fully alive.

As we [Sister Josephine and I] were writing the manual for the Beginning Experience Program, we were discussing the real need, especially for women, to perceive themselves as whole individuals, especially in the divorce situation where the majority of people feel half of something. The half that was strong, was aggressive, was capable and so on, has left, and they see themselves as the other half. The first tendency is to go out and to get that back, wearing a different face or something. But what's really needed is to perceive that you have within yourself the capability to be a whole person.

Part of the problem comes from the programming. As children we are not brought up to perceive ourselves, especially as girls, as growing into totally capable, whole individuals. If you have that idea already, then you can reach out to someone in a really healthy way and say to that person, "Together we can be more than we are separate."

We need to do something to provide our children with some insights that too often are lost until they have already made some major decisions. All the knowledge we teach them about math and science isn't enough and can't be unified into a happy life unless they have some basic knowledge and understanding of themselves and human nature. That's my hope for kids of the future, as a way of life: to really have a belief in yourself and your ability. I think boys were brought up to believe they could do certain things, but they really weren't as good as girls in sensitivity and compassion and showing feelings or emotions. And girls were brought up with permission to be strong in certain areas, but only certain ones . . . and I think unconsciously we, women my age, have thought that.

I've done a lot of thinking about the past and who I was before my first marriage. I've been looking for danger signs that perhaps I had put aside, and wondering what caused me to overlook those signs. I think it was probably social pressures: that your goal in life is to find a husband and get married. I was working at the fire department the first time I met my husband. We started dating for about a year, and there were personality traits that I didn't like in him. But I could rationalize anything away, and I looked at the positive things and found excuses for the negative ones with an almost desperate feeling that this is the one chance and somehow this has got to work out right.

The strongest attraction to him was emotional and common sense. Also, I was flattered because he was nine years older than I was, and had done a lot of traveling, and here I was so much younger. I think it was the flattery. I had never dated much, and I really didn't have much experience. I had ideas of my own about what I didn't like, but very little practical experience to see if that was too idealistic. I had ideas that I would like a husband to be kind, considerate, and all these things, but in rationalizing, I thought, no one is perfect. I think I was somewhat intimidated by him because he was a very strong individual, which I didn't feel I was. I saw myself as weak and independent. So there were good parts I was missing.

I think I saw marriage as a fulfillment. I wanted a good Christian marriage, in which God would play an important part and in which the children would grow up happy, probably ideals gathered from reading. I was a real dreamer. I was a National Honor Society scholarship winner, but since there was no money in the family at that time, my award was saved for my younger brother's education, I didn't go to college. I got a job as a secretary and was really bored. So I thought fulfillment for me would be in marriage, as wife and mother.

I was from a sheltered Catholic background, and he said after our first date, "You're the girl I want to marry." I'm sure he was delighted with my background. When he asked me if I had ever thought of marrying a non-Catholic I said, "No, it seems to cause a lot of problems." Well, he went to the library and did a lot of reading on the Catholic Church and signed up for instructions, apart from me. He was an intelligent man and said this was what he wanted to do. That made a big impression on me. He was very much aware of how important my religion was to me, and I was very much rules and regulations, probably too scrupulous.

One time, about a month before the wedding, his drinking got out of hand and I sensed he was seeing me as an object. I had ceased to be a person and that frightened me, so I got out of the car and started walking home. I gave him back his ring, but I had the pressure of the wedding invitations already being out. Also, he called the next day and was really mopping up the floor with apologies, and swore that it was only the liquor, so I laid that aside. From time to time, I was aware that I was uncomfortable in that relationship, but just thought that I was being unrealistic—you know, too idealistic. So the wedding went on. But things really did start getting worse. Before my first son was born, I had left him and gone home.

In my mind I had worked out that when we were married everything would be all right. As long as you had a good attitude, whatever happened between husband and wife was part of God's plan for that marriage. I assumed I would have no problem with the sex part of it, and I didn't though it was very, very important to Virgil. However, I think emotionally I was feeling somewhat empty, and having nothing to compare it to, I thought I was a real dreamer thinking that sex should have been a more loving, caring sort of thing. I began to think he really didn't love and care about me as a person, only as a woman. I was disillusioned. I thought marriage was a special relationship between two people, not a physical relationship between opposite sexes. I just wasn't honest enough with myself or aware enough to realize that the things that were needed to make that kind of relationship weren't present.

The divorce came fourteen years after the marriage. All those years were struggles. The first seven I prayed constantly, expecting God to send a thunderbolt. After seven years I began to become discouraged and found I wasn't saint material. In my readings, saints found joy in their sufferings, and there was none in mine. I decided to start putting things together, to do some reading and start facing what my children were being brought up in and what I was living in. I was reading psychology and spiritual books: Fromm's *The Art of Loving*, Roger's *On Becoming a Person*, and Missildine's *Your Inner Child of the Past*. Some were really helpful in understanding why I was staying in the situation. The church wasn't a support. From time to time the priest simply said, "Go back and try harder." Well, I did, and it wasn't getting any better. I just became more and more miserable. Eight years of marriage and I wanted to leave after having three children right in a row. I had no money, Virgil was completely in control of the material things. I hadn't worked in seven years. My parents said, "You're crazy. You have a roof over your head and a steady income. Try harder."

I think I grew stronger in those years, but it came to the point where I would have to admit that I was crazy, because I had changed as much as I could according to his wishes. He was always using scripture: "A wife is dutiful to her husband," and so on. I don't think he had really any religion. He stopped going to the Catholic church the first year of our marriage because the priest drank beer. That was just an excuse. He wanted me to give up completely and say, "You are right. I am a really rotten person and I should be grateful for your letting me stay," which was the message I had been getting. Nothing I did was right. He was becoming so negative and the pressures got so bad I began to believe I was mentally ill.

I was saying things I thought were smart, out of all this reading and all of my willingness to be honest. Things like, "I don't understand how I can get along so well with other people and not him." He assured me that no one else saw how really rotten I was. He said I was lucky he let me stay there. After all that negative programming for ten years, I had to find out how much of a person in me was left, if any. So one day in desperation I called my mother and asked for twenty dollars to go and see a counselor. He pulled the ignition wires out and took the car keys, but I still made it to the counselor. I knew I wouldn't have any more money, so I typed out this history and talked as fast as I could for one hour. And the counselor said, "I think your marriage has a problem. You're not mentally ill, but I need to see your husband." As I was walking out the door he said, "If your husband won't come and you want to see what you want for yourself, then you come back." And that scared me, scared me more than trying to talk Virgil into coming to see the counselor.

When I went home there was a big crisis. He had all the kids in tears and was going to sell the furniture off. I found whatever I did being used against the kids. But it gave me a ray of hope that someone had said, "You are thinking some good things; you're not mentally ill." That was the beginning of physical persecution in the process, but it was the strengthening of the person.

I was abused to the point of finally filing for a divorce in 1972. The whole previous year some really sick things had been happening on and off. It reminded me of the nursery rhyme about the little girl who had written on her forehead, "When she was good she was very, very good, and when she was bad she was horrid." He was drinking, but emotionally he was also on edge. Our house looked like a mass evacuation at 4:30 when all the kids' friends poured out. We would have liked to leave too. Even my relatives stopped coming. But at the same time in my own life, with P.T.A. and different organizations, I was feeling more confident about myself. That was really very destructive to that relationship, because the only way it would have survived was if I had become nothing.

So I filed for divorce, and he took a gun and was going to kill my lawyer. Then suddenly he reversed and agreed to a counselor. He used my need for God against me. There were four months of reconciliation that were really crazy: a gun at my head, a knife at my throat, choking me, throwing me across the room. I went to the counselor, who said, "Get back there, he's not going to kill you. Work things out." I was seeing the counselor three times a week until he finally quit. He said I was becoming paranoid with him so he couldn't help me. The counselor asked me if I wanted to be paid back for all my misery, and that is exactly what I was feeling, so I felt like a selfish person. I was aware that if I became bitter and hated him, I would be hurting myself. The persecution continued on a daily basis. My lawyer had me keep a journal to bring to court. Anyone who came to my house was harrassed. I tried so hard to accept and forgive. I knew he was sick, and I thought I would just work on not hating him.

After a slow and painful process, I feel I got that far, but much more healing is needed. The injuries were so deep. A lot of healing took place last year with the Beginning, but for me that is just a beginning. One real wound was that for a time I had to send all of my children to a home. My crisis isn't over because of the divorce. We live with reminders. My oldest daughter needs to see how she feels about her father before she cannot let that get in the way of other relationships, as it is now. Authority figures and any kind of father figure are a real threat to her. When Christopher came, he did a final parting with his father. He was about to get bashed in the head with a crowbar and decided it might be smarter to leave. When anything upsets Virgil, he threatens to kill me, even now. But I don't feel I can waste today in worrying about whether he is ever going to come up here and find me, or what he would do. Today my life is good, and I trust that.

If I could give my son a gift after all these years, I would give him an acceptance of his sensitivity. He was a sensitive child, and he was spanked, beaten, whipped from the time he was ten months old for crying, because boys don't cry. Virgil believes a man is strong and crying is a weakness. Christopher can still cry, and I was so happy for him when I saw that. He had a girlfriend in Texas he had to leave behind when he came here. He couldn't return because of his father; he would have had to carry a knife or gun. So it was an emotional decision on his part. When Jerry asked him to stay here, there was a lot of pain in separating himself from his girlfriend, and he cried. I thought that was probably the most hopeful sign, that he could still be real.

Jerry was a neighbor of mine. After the divorce he called from time to time. His wife was in a sanitarium. We had the same values. Getting his own head straight was important to him. He was caring and sensitive. Love began to grow for each other, along with the feeling we both had about how important it was to be a whole person. By being honest and becoming more of a person, there was more to give to other people.

When I came out of the divorce I had no one: no family, no friends. There was a whole year of isolation when the threats were very real and were carried out against anyone who had anything to do with me. After the divorce, I was advised to get the children out of the area because the judge was going to issue a writ taking away Virgil's parental rights. They felt that when they did that he would go berserk and kill all of us. That is when I sent the children to the Methodist Home. If Virgil had exploded then, things would have been resolved sooner, but he began to see a psychiatrist and it dragged on for ten months, during which I could see the children twice a month. At that time Virgil started programming the boys: boys raised by their mothers would become homosexual and so on. He followed me and threatened me, and I really was alone. But during that time I really came to know what was important to me. I wrote like crazy, even when the whole world was upside down.

Jerry came along as a friend I could talk to. The wounded ministering to the wounded. He was someone saying, "Yes, I didn't have similar experiences, but I felt this way." I was very leery of our friendship. I knew I was becoming a person, but I wasn't at all interested in testing that. My understanding of marriage was give and give, and how can you do that and take care of another person's needs and still remain an individual and growing in regard to your own needs? So when our relationship grew stronger and stronger and the subject of marriage did come up, I really thought it was ironic. As much as I had avoided divorce, with all the tears and so on, in a similar way I was turning away from the idea of marriage again. It seemed like such a dangerous thing to do, because I wasn't sure if you could really have a loving, giving, fulfilling marriage and remain two individual persons.

So I did more reading and more writing. God was the main reason I survived. In trying to get my oldest daughter's ideas straightened out, we did an evaluation a couple of months ago, and what came out of it was the psychiatrist's comment that he wanted to do a study of me to find out why I am still alive, because I should have been killed. I really believe that it was the grace of God that I wasn't killed on several occaions, when I should have been just from the circumstances of a loaded gun that was cocked and a bottle of vodka in the other hand. I did what I could to survive, but I know that it was the grace of God.

It started about two years before the divorce. So I credit the strengthening of that—well, I was at a loss for words, words not given to me in my Catholic upbringing, but it was really a direct experience of God. A personal experience that grew into a personal relationship. Also, I thought how handicapped I was, because Catholics aren't really taught that there is something else to find. I thought God to be important to me all my life, but I thought you found him by keeping the rules and regulations, and if there was a distance, it was because you weren't keeping them well enough.

Prayer up to that time was mostly novenas that had guarantees. It never dawned on me to say that all those printed guarantees were wrong. For some reason I never came to the point of saying the church was all wrong. I judged myself as lacking. I found God out of despair, I guess. It was at the point when I was taking my husband seriously that I was rotten and no good. I was so far down I said, "Okay, maybe that is how I am." Out of that time I had the feeling of God saying, "Even if you are, I still love you. It wouldn't matter to me if you were nothing. If you had no talents, no gifts, I created you and that is enough. I love you." Accepting that and agreeing to try to find out who I was, I began to look in hope.

At the time of this personal experience there was such an exchange of thoughts and ideas that it was totally different from anything I had thought of. I found myself talking with God as a friend. Sometimes it was in my writing. I was very aware that it was a prayer, and how different that was from what I was brought up on. The survival during those two or three years was also a real spiritual growth, as well as a real persecution.

A good friend who helped me was a Baptist. Another was a priest who shared with me that he had been a priest for thirteen years before he had a similar experience. He was a real human. He was an affirmation for me, and he was a Catholic saying the same thing my Baptist friend said. The relationship between God and me was so personal that I didn't need to rush out and put a label on it. I continued to go to mass, to do reading, and to find people who were real spiritual people for me. It began to be unimportant to me what people called themselves, but it was important how they lived.

When my children were gone, I developed a pattern that I still continue now. I go away by myself and see what I think and feel, talking to God about it and writing. I tell the children I need this time. If I don't do it for a day or two, I can feel the difference. It's like distancing myself from myself and from God. Praying, a time for me of conversation with God, and meditation, which is me shutting up and just being there in whatever mood I am in, this was very necessary to me. This was hard for me, because I was brought up to think emotionalist was Protestant. And because I was personally involved with God, I was aware some people would call me a religious fanatic. But I was so desperate I didn't have a choice.

The psychiatrist that was helping me was also trying to put together a theology of the battered wife. He had eight such patients at the time, and he wanted to find something to help them help themselves. He was trying to understand my thinking process and what had helped me to get off myself in the first place. When nothing was working out, when I couldn't do anymore, it was my spiritual life that was giving me the energy to go on. I think what any woman has to do is to make the decision to be a person. It must be done in a balanced way, but it isn't a selfless decision. As long as I saw myself as a creature of God that was loved and had value . . . without that it might seem easier to stay. The change is threatening. All the things I scared myself with, Virgil reinforced, and I was saying, "Yes, he must be right." Without having had the spiritual experience, that I was not completely worthless, that there was some good in me, that God loves me, I would not have survived.

Jerry and I were coordinators for the north region of Beginnings, a weekend that was designed for the divorced, separated, or widowed. It has grown, and so has the work. We have five children; two of Jerry's, three of mine. It's like three families together. My younger son and my daughter came with me when we married, and Jerry's two children came with him. About eighteen months ago, when my older son came, it was like a third family joining us. It had been four years since we had seen or heard from him. There's been a lot of time and energy spent trying to work out the difficulties involved in having people from that many different backgrounds joined together and have a family feeling, because that was very important. My children had been through so much disruption. I had decided there wasn't anything I could do to change the past, but not to use the suffering constructively would make a waste of all of it. So I guess I was really determined to make something good for the children out of those bad experiences, because each of them came with different nightmares.

I don't see the Beginnings as work, but more as a spiritual commitment, because it came out of my life's experience. It wasn't what I set out to do, but what I went through and my feelings are important to other people, to help them understand their own feelings and to accept them. During the times when all the bad things were happening, it was hard for me to ever see any good coming out of it. Yet I would not be in such a position to help people in all varieties of crisis now if it had not been for my own history and deaths. I can help women through my sharing. That is what I saw as the value in contributing to your book: just a few phrases about how I find myself effective in working with people who maybe have no image of themselves, short phrases that say what was true for me and what I hung on to while everything else was crazy. It doesn't have to be complicated. It's simple and it's real, and they can hold on to it, too. It doesn't mean that you have to plow through chapters of psychology and scripture. The God and the spirituality I started experiencing were very different from my memory of the catechism God.

I became a married woman again, we moved up here, and I was seen differently than I had been two days before in Texas. There I was a divorced woman, and here all people knew was that a new family had moved into town. There was a husband, a wife, and children. I had the choice of joining a women's club or the Beginnings movement, and I did join the women's club at first. I thought that would be a good way to get to meet people, and I did want to be open to a regular family life because I was very aware that my life there had been so pressured. I wasn't seen as different now, yet I felt different from most of the married women I'd met. I judged things that they weren't thinking about to be important: being honest with myself and how I feel and think, and being honest with my husband and with my kids. I was sure the way I survived was by praying and making God an important part of my life, and I was always aware I had survived because of God's strength assisting me.

JO DORR   *(Boston, Massachusetts.) Occupation: Professor in the School of Nursing, Boston University; lecturer on aging and death; community health nurse. Age: 41. Education: M.S. in community health nursing.*

Divorced; two daughters.

I am a community health care nurse, and that is my first love. I have done a lot of taking care of the elderly. If I had my choice, I would love to work mostly with old people. Working with the aged and dying and helping people to do creative aging is a form of reconciliation. I am an Episcopalian, and the idea of reconciliation was always negative for me. It conveyed resignation rather than acceptance. It relates, I think, a lot to what I see in terms of decision-making and other chances at any point in life, especially midlife. I really believe that we are more today because we've lived this day, as well as because we've had some losses. There is always the chance to reconcile what it is we are with what we were and what we can become.

I do see it in relation to another chance, not just a second chance, but continuously another chance to make some new decisions, to make some changes, to decide that this is not the kind of person I really want to be. How can I keep changing? For me, when I can get myself to the point where the spotlight is not on me, then I can truly focus on other people, for instance patients. There I can really listen loudly to people, and touch them and let them touch me. This takes inner resources, and for me that has to do with listening to music, or better yet, playing music with nobody around. That is like *rebirth*.

I started teaching evening courses so I could go to school by day and teach by night. Some of my students got frustrated because they wanted to spend longer with me, so I developed an undergraduate course called "The Sociology of the Middle Years." I was scared to death because I hadn't done any original research in the area of the middle years, but we tried it out and it was a dynamite experience for me.

I started sharing what I knew as well as learning what they knew, and it is attracting all kinds of people, from young people who want to understand their parents to parents who want to understand the young people. I guess you could call it "passages." It has to do with what happens to us, regardless of whether we are single, married, male, or female, in passing through the middle years of our life. What are some of the issues? What are some of the things that we impose on ourselves based upon how we were reared, as well as some of the things society says we ought to be doing, or we should have done by now? How does that affect our health, our well-being? How do we age gracefully? Creatively? We cover the biological, the psychological, and the sociological, because it makes the course legitimate. Then we do the spiritual, and just whatever is meaningful to creative aging. I use resources and people who have gotten themselves through some of their crises and who can see where the threads have been. People like Mary Richards and her book *Centering*.

There have been unexpected things happening, especially in the "Death and Mourning" course. Our Ma died. She was our mother in the sense that she came when Sandy was an infant and had been with us for all those years. She was like the mother I never had and the mother my kids missed because I was working. I advertised in the paper and she appeared and said, "Well, you need me and I need you," and she just came in and started to work the next day.

I didn't want to begin the death course because I was in such pain. I went in and I had to share what was happening, because otherwise I never really would have touched base with them. I learned from them, but the pain was intense. I had grown a lot personally. Dealing in the area of aging and death, I learned the art of living in keeping up in my personal relationships. Ma knew I loved her, and I knew she loved me, and my kids knew it too. There wasn't any unfinished business—no guilt. She left us with such gifts.

Her death was a turning point. My husband and I had decided not to live together, and Ma was a part of that. She knew it, she understood it, she accepted it. When she died, I was able to give myself permission to let go of the marriage. Nineteen years I had been hanging on. We were really good friends, but we could never recapture the marriage. The friendship began long before we became intimate, and it will last long years after. It was a creative divorce, but like death, like anything where there is loss and/or gain, it involved a certain amount of grieving. I don't feel drawn into trying to reestablish an intimate relationship with him. It's been too many years, and

I can't back up. His and my spirituality have become different now. To me, spirituality is knowing your central core of values and giving yourself permission to accept these in a way that doesn't inhibit further growth.

I am really a loner in many ways, and I need a lot of private time. I need a lot of space, and without it I get to the point where I really want to kill myself. I have hideouts where I hang out, and I don't tell anybody. Wherever I can find that other people are not, I go there. I teach intense courses, and I need to get away from the telephones.

I think about grace a lot of those times, because I have people who make me think about it. I am constantly aware of feeling very fortunate and thanking something bigger than myself for where I am. Some of the people I am exposed to are very well and very active, and some are ready to die and are in the state of grace. They literally are conscious at all times of feeling the sense of thanks for what they have, and even welcoming whatever else happens to them.

I don't pray in a conscious "kneel-down-and-pray" way, but I've always got a prayer in my head or in my heart; not in words, but in feeling. I grew up in the church even though I don't go now, and I have a deep love for music. When I least expect it, I will sing a hymn that was meaningful to me when I grew up. I had a very unhappy childhood, and my two saving graces were school and church music.

My focus now in teaching is on the changes that occur in aging. They represent losses as well as increments. I want to enrich the study of aging. Aging is change, and change is giving up the self we once knew. I can reconcile the losses I feel so far, because I am forty and nothing drastic has happened to me. I still do the things I like to do; in fact, I do most of them better than ever. We know more cells die than are born every day, but so far that hasn't interfered with anything. I am even kind of glad to get rid of some.

I work with people of all generations and I watch what happens. I have hope in people who are filled with grace, who feel better and better about themselves. They are reconciled. I want to just capture them for a moment and find out what it is that has brought them meaning; what is it that has made them feel the way they do. How have they done that when there are invitations all over the place in our society to be suicidal, physically and mentally! What is the will to live versus the will to die?

I am devoting much of my time outside of academia to the hospice movement. We have a little community outside of Boston to help families be comfortable in allowing the person who is doing the dying to live until they die. If there is grieving to be done, we help them in such a way that it doesn't abort the person who is dying. The family is often so emotionally involved *doing* the dying that they've said their goodbyes already and have let go while the person is still alive. It's hard, especially if it is a long-term thing, and sometimes an outsider can help a family see what's going on and shift gears. Part of that work is of course dealing with aging. It gives us great *hope* to see people age and die with grace, feeling better about themselves, welcoming whatever happens to them.

If we really want to help older persons, we have to find out what they were like before they hit the school system, what other people remember about them, what things turned them on, how they were before they got their creativity drummed out of them. They usually don't know: they have been so beautifully socialized. Where did the meaning in life come from before we started to rearrange it and categorize it and put it into slots? It seems to me that when I did my own graduate work they were trying to drum out all the originality in order to satisfy the requirements.

We need each other. It's an intergenerational thing. There is no population of elderly women, or men, but rather a group of people we call that. The interchange is essential. It is an invitation to living, and I worry whenever people segregate themselves, whether it is men or women, young or old. We need each other, but we are raised from an early age in our society to be independent after having come from total dependencies, and nowhere along the way are we taught anything about becoming interdependent. What a bleak outlook for me, if I move through my time and space and get to where they are and don't have any interchange whereby they are allowed to give me their gifts as well as my doing what I can for them.

PAMELA ST. DENIS *(Scituate, Massachusetts.) Student at Boston University in Jo Dorr's Death and Dying class; writer.*

Separated mother who has lost two of five children to crib death.

I would like to thank my seventeen-year-old sister-in-law, Margaret St. Denis, for helping me write this story. Every time I would start to write, the pain and hurt would make me stop. Because she listened and encouraged me to keep on writing, I feel a weight has been lifted off me. Together we cried and made it possible for this story to be written. Thank you, Margaret.

I am just starting to try to put my life into perspective after three years of tragic loss. Two of my children died of sudden infant death syndrome, better known as crib death. Crib death is a disease of unknown etiology that kills eight to ten thousand babies a year. There is no warning when this disease strikes. A baby is put to bed and dies in its sleep. Crib death has no preference as to race, color, or environment, and was mentioned even in the Bible.

To lose one's healthy, beautiful child without warning is a terrible shock. The aftermath of trying to accept what happened is almost like a disease itself. Because so little is known about crib death, the majority of people in our society have never heard of this disease. When most people hear of a baby dying for no apparent reason, it is very hard for them not to suspect negligence on the part of the parent. I speak from experience, since I hold within me pain, bitterness, and hostility as a consequence of society's ignorance of the unknown. After three years of holding in emotions, which I had been conditioned was the proper thing to do, the depression and sadness of the loss of two beautiful baby daughters is starting to overpower my strength of mind.

After having reared two healthy daughters, Elizabeth, five, and Naomi, three, I gave birth to what appeared to be another healthy baby girl. My husband Carl and I had been having our marital problems, and when Rachel was born she brought us closer together. It was the first time Carl had participated in the birth of one of our children. Rachel had deep blue eyes and black hair, a really beautiful child. For three months Carl and I shared changing diapers, making formula, feeding Rachel, and loving every minute of it.

One afternoon I was driving Carl to work and Rachel was in the car bed in the back of the car. After dropping my husband off, I went home and thought she had fallen off to sleep. I gently carried the car bed up the stairs to our apartment. Rachel had a bunting on, and even though I was going to be going out again, I didn't want her to be too warm. I lifted her from the car bed, and she went limp in my arms.

Unreality hit me like a bolt of lightning. I started to shake her, and I could hear an ungodly scream which was my own. Somewhere in the depths of my mind I recalled the mouth-to-mouth resuscitation I had been taught in high school. I quickly began to administer it as best I could. My downstairs neighbor came running through the door, and somehow in the confusion the fire department was called. It seemed like an eternity before they came.

Rachel lived for eighteen hours because of my efforts and the heroics of the fire department. Carl and I left the hospital too numb to fall apart. When we reached the car, he put his arms around me and told me we were lucky we still had two children. I wanted to scream at him that I didn't care about the other children, I just wanted my baby back in my arms. I have often thought about that statement, and it has bothered me that I could have even thought that I felt that way.

The funeral was a fiasco, now that I think back. I was told just to bury her quietly with no flowers and no church mass. To this day I think of how my family and friends reacted, as though my daughter's death was a relatively insignificant event. What I wouldn't have given for just one family member or friend to come and sit with me at night and let me cry my heart out.

This may sound a little self-pitying, but had I gotten over my sorrow and mourned Rachel at the time of her death, I might now be able to cope better. My husband was no emotional support. Carl was not able to handle the situation, and walked out when I found myself three months pregnant with a fourth child. At first I was upset about the pregnancy, but, not believing in abortion, I accepted and anticipated the birth of a new baby.

At the time, there was a group of young boys, aged eighteen to twenty, who hung out on the corner of my street. I hardly knew them when Rachel died, although I had been living in the neighborhood for three years. They came one night with a booklet enrolling Rachel in six daily masses for eternity and signed it, "From the boys on the corner." To me this was a very touching and beautiful experience, as none of my other neighbors had even told me they were sorry. What their reasons were for staying away when I needed them most I will never fully understand.

Three weeks before I delivered, I had a small breakdown. My doctors put me in the hospital because I was too anxious over the birth of my new baby. I was really frightened. Could they guarantee me it would not happen again? Yes, they told me it would not happen again, because it was rare for two children in the same family to die of crib death.

When I delivered a nine-pound, healthy, beautiful baby girl, I was ecstatic. If I had had a son, I would have been disappointed, because I was trying to replace the baby I had lost. In my mind, Fawn did replace Rachel. They looked so much alike; they even had the same exact point in their left ear. The excitement of having a new baby brought me and my other two children closer together. Elizabeth could feed and change Fawn, and Naomi would run and get the diaper or the powder. They both knew and understood in their childish way that this was a special baby. Several times they asked me if Fawn would die, and each time I would tell them no, because God wouldn't take her away from us.

After Rachel's death, the children and I started to see a psychologist. Elizabeth refused to discuss Rachel's death because she told the doctor it made me cry. I am a very lucky woman, because the gift of my children's love is a special treasure. They were always checking on Fawn while she napped, and this they did on their own. I think sometimes children sense more than we give them credit for.

Then it happened. After five joy-filled months of love, sudden infant death quietly and maliciously took my beautiful Fawn away from me. We were to go on a picnic because it was the Fourth of July. When I awoke a terrible feeling came over me, and I was afraid to move out of the bed. For some reason I knew Fawn was dead. I walked over to her cradle and knew with just one look that she was gone. I couldn't touch her. I couldn't help her. I just screamed and screamed, "God, help me please." Of course God could not help me. I had to help myself. I called Carl at his apartment and told him to come quickly, the baby was dead. He made it just in time, before the ambulance pulled away. To this day, whenever I hear a siren, my heart beats a little faster.

At the hospital I remember my husband saying that it wasn't our child and it couldn't have happened again. Somehow, almost unbelievably, I heard myself tell him that it was our baby and she was dead, and we would have to accept it. I looked at her still form lying there in the emergency room and gently touched her. Even in death, she was still beautiful.

This time I was going to have flowers and this time there was going to be a church mass. I couldn't believe I was making these decisions and I didn't give a damn about family or friends. I don't really know what good all this did, but it gave me some peace of mind to know that it was the last thing I could ever give to her.

Even though Rachel and Fawn were infants when they died, they were still a part of me. I had felt them grow inside of me. When they died, a part of me died with them, and no amount of comfort, condolence, or therapy will ever give back that which has been taken away from me. I started attending crib-death meetings after Fawn's death, hoping to find support and understanding. All I found was a lot of bitterness and confusion among other parents. Needless to say, I stopped attending. Maybe I just wasn't ready for these meetings.

When I found out I was pregnant with a fifth child, I couldn't believe it, and I did contemplate having an abortion. A woman who worked closely with a doctor researching crib death at the Massachusetts General Hospital called me to tell me she had lost a baby from crib death and that her subsequent child had been put on a monitor and was doing well. The monitor would be available to me if I wanted it. I felt relief and gratitude because the thought of the monitor made my pregnancy bearable.

When the doctor held up my baby girl and laid her on my stomach, I cried and sobbed. I was afraid to touch her and get close to her because there was no guarantee on her life as far as I was concerned. It took me two days to muster up enough courage to see her. She didn't even have a name until a girlfriend of mine told me to name her Hope because all I had to hang on to was hope.

They brought Hope down to me from intensive care. I had disoriented myself from reality and couldn't believe I had another baby. The nurses were very kind, and when they put Hope in my arms, we all cried together. It was really beautiful to have people care and know that they meant it.

Hope is fifteen months old now and ready to come off the monitor, but I'm not ready to make that decision yet because I don't want to be another rare case and lose her. The doctors can't guarantee me that crib death won't be repeated. They have statistics, but I don't want to be that one out of ten thousand again. I feel alone and hostile, and I'd rather be safe than sorry in keeping Hope on the monitor. It is going to take a while for me to deal with this situation. I never feel alone with the monitor, and I wake up several times at night just to watch the light blink, showing she is breathing. When the monitor goes, I will be losing a friend that got me through rough waters. Just the thought of not having it around to reassure me is frightening. I cannot afford to lose anything that I love and trust right now, whether it be material or immaterial.

When I wake up in the morning and Hope reaches out her little arms to me with that sweet, trusting, innocent smile, I say to myself, "Damn you, know-it-all doctors, go to hell. I'll take her off when I'm damn good and ready."

MARIE IRENE LOWLEY *Flathead Indian Reservation, Tensed, Idaho. Age: 58. Daughter and granddaughter of chiefs of the Coeur d'Alene tribe.*

Widowed; mother of seven, grand-mother of nineteen, great-grand-mother of one.

I didn't care for the expression that Indians are "savages," so I wrote this and put it under the title, "I Wonder Why?" It goes like this:

The heritage of our Indians should be taught with the same respect as that of the "great white leaders" of yesteryear. The native American Indians are a proud nation. Is it so hard to give them honor in the same breath as the white nation, who did come into Indian country for only one purpose: to form a self-government free of all dominating ties with the Old World? My people could not understand why these strange people came into their midst and said, "These are our lands, and you savages are the intruders." We were stripped of our rights to hunt and fish and breathe the clean air, to drink the sweet, clear waters from the mountain streams and rest under the spreading leaves of the great pine, fir, tamarack, oak, and willow trees. Today my people are still suffering from the loss of their lands and the purity of the air which made them strong in mind and HEART. How can anyone say, "These are the savages who ripped off my people"? I would say with all truth of HEART and loss, that we will wonder until the end of time what happened to us, the great American people, the American Indian.

As I sit in front of this picture window, my mind goes back to when I was a child and the beauty of the mountain top, the wooded earth, the blue sky. I can remember my grandmother saying, "Early in the morning, after I attend mass, I am leaving for a while to gather my food for the winter. When the sun sets three Sundays from tomorrow, I will be back. You children mind your father and oldest sister. And do not make your father unhappy because he will be tired when he comes in from clearing the land and

*will want to eat his supper and smoke his cigarette and go to bed
early so he can get up early and go back into the field." Does this
sound like a savage speaking to her grandchildren? Her first
thought is the welfare and comfort of her son and his children.*

I am the granddaughter and daughter of a chief of the Coeur
d'Alene tribe, and when you were selected to be chief, you were the
head of the tribe. Any problems that came up, it was felt the chief
had to help them with, married life problems and things like that. If
it was deeper than they thought the chief could help them with, they
went to see Father Byrnes. They appointed my father chief because
he had been the son of a chief. The younger generation wanted a
younger chief, so they overruled the older generation. The younger
men said they would like to have him as chief because he would
understand the young as well as understanding the older folks.

My own thoughts of my childhood are beautiful. I am the youngest of five children. My father and mother were separated. She
divorced my father, and he got custody of all the children. We were
raised by my grandmother and my older sister, who at the time was
eleven years old.

My relationship with my dad was beautiful. Words can't express
my feelings toward him. He was stern, but so understanding. I spent
all my days with him until he passed away. I left for a while when
my mother took me; sometimes I think it was out of spite because
she knew how attached I was to my dad. She did take me to
Montana, where she's from, and left me with her mother. I stayed
there with her until I got very ill. The doctors found out I was home-
sick, and no medicine on earth could cure me except my dad,
brothers, and sisters. And so I came back and have been here ever
since, except during the war, when I worked in Spokane.

I might be putting this too strong, but I always had the feeling
mother didn't mind having babies, but didn't want the responsibility
of raising them. I couldn't wait to have children, and when I had my
seven, I loved the first as much as I did the last one I had. I had a
routine with my children that didn't exhaust me to tears. I took
good care of my children; they hardly ever had to go to the doctor.

My grandmother taught us how to cook a simple meal, take care
of the house, and look after the children while my dad and she were
out clearing the land on her place, which was her allotment when
the Allotment Act came in. My grandfather, Chief Saltiz, died before
the allotment, so he was not allowed a share. Grandmother was the
only one; my dad wasn't allowed, too young. All I can remember is

the beautiful stories my grandmother would tell my younger brother and me after school before prayer time. She always dimmed her light at nine o'clock and said her night prayer every night. That used to be a family thing with all of us when granddad was alive.

The difference between my grandmother and me was that she loved the outdoors and I loved doing inside-the-house things. I cooked three hot meals for my children while they were home, and if they were at school I had supper ready for them at 4:30. But as for tender loving care, my grandmother was just overflowing with it. She disciplined us, and then she'd weep after she did and ask us not to be naughty so she'd have to discipline us again. Not once did she ever belittle my mother for leaving us.

As time went by, we lost grandma, and my older sister continued to raise us and be our sister at the same time. She left to get married when she was pretty close to thirty. I stayed with my dad up until his death in 1949.

Then I married in 'fifty. I was married almost seven years when I became widowed. I didn't have much of an income, so I was on state aid for a while when all my children were small. We had seven of them. After they got big, they went on to school here at the Convent of Mary Magdalene, taught by the Sisters of Charity of Providence. I am now a grandmother of nineteen and great-grandmother of one. My own children don't come to see me very often. Two of my girls are far away. They both married Nez Perce men.

I have never remarried. My husband was a hard-working man, for many relatives other than his own mother. He worked on the farm when he was twelve for room and board only. He was in the defense program during the war. When we got married, I told him being a housewife in the city was not my idea of homelife, so I wanted to live in the country. We tried farm work, but the machinery was so expensive. He worked hard, but I don't mean he was a saintly man. He liked his beer and he liked his weekends at the tavern. In fact, he was coming home when he was killed, hit and run. The coroner said there wasn't a bone in his body that wasn't broken, he was hit with such impact.

That was in 1957. We would have been married seven years that fall. I think a stepchild is something I never wanted my children to be, so I never remarried. When I saw my husband crumpled up on the side of the highway I made that promise to him, that I would never remarry and would raise our children and give all of my time to them and not to anyone else.

When I was working I got along real well with everybody. One time they asked me what nationality I was, and I said, "I'm not a nationality, I'm an American Indian, and my ancestors were here before any of you." They laughed it off and never held it against me. I never had the problem of racial prejudice, and for that I was quite lucky. I was accepted for the work I could do.

I have been lonely. Many times I thought, "What am I doing home? I am still quite young. I could still be with some companion and go to a movie or a dinner or something." Then I'd think of my kids, and that would snap me out of it just like that. And prayers! Believe you me, I prayed for strength to keep the promise I made.

I had no friends, just one lady that would come and visit me. She would be tired—she was a cook at the restaurant—and she would fall asleep. If she woke up, she would go home in the night. Or she'd stay until day and go back to work. She did shopping for me once in a while. Sometimes I would hire someone with a car. I wasn't too shy to do that. On Sunday, we'd get ready early and walk to mass, my kids and me.

Our lives intermingled with everybody's when we went to church. We'd stop and greet everybody, and if there was any sadness among our friends, we'd give our condolences and our prayers. This mission is a tightly grouped place. Nothing is important until it happens here on this Sacred Heart Mission. We have several buildings: an elementary school and a public gathering place.

Thank God we were healthy enough not to make a nuisance of ourselves with my friends. Most of the time I occupied myself with my duties toward my children and my home. When the kids would be taking a nap I would do the laundry every day, and patchwork, and ironing, cooking, or darning, and time for myself just worked in.

Now I work here at the school every day. I go home and have a light supper. My grandson changes clothes all the time, so I've got wash every day. I pull a few weeds around my flower bed, clean my parakeet's cage, watch TV. Once in a while I stop at my younger son's trailer and see the kids. I've got my routines. Not very exciting, is it?

My hope for the future? Our young people are going on to higher education, masters' and so on. I was a dropout. I have the experience, but I don't have the education. It will get them ordinary day-to-day living, and probably boredom, which happens to everyone. Time has gone by. We say, Tomorrow we can do it. Tomorrow is such, such a short time.

MARGE HUGHES *(A mountaintop near Hamlin, West Virginia.) Occupations: Presently working on the Hamlin newspaper staff; former Catholic Worker; former coadministrator of Tivoli Farm with Peter Maurin and Dorothy Day. Age: 68. Education: Self-educated.*

Divorced mother of four children.

All my life, I think my three basic preoccupations have been with poverty, love, and freedom. Along with that, I had these very absolute notions of what was required—a sort of legalistic mind, you know, what you must do and what you must not do. I had a lot of feelings of inadequacy, that the musts were not being fulfilled, and a lot of feelings of guilt that I was doing things that I shouldn't do. There was a split, in other words, between my awareness of my religion as a social force, of what possible contribution I could make there, and of what direction I felt one should go in in the area of freedom and love and poverty and service and being one with people. Somehow that was split off from spiritual life, which was involved with how you were fulfilling the law or the commandments or the beatitudes or whatever. It was all made into law in my head, into absolutes, and it took me a long time to get those things sorted out and get them together.

The older I get, the more I am convinced that you don't really know very much about what you were meant to be. You have to somehow allow the spirit to form you; be open to the spirit, and everything else will flow from that with spontaneity. Thought isn't enough: the spirit must be part of it too. You think about things and at the same time try to withdraw projections. For me that's where it is.

I think that the most truly detached person is the most open to perception of another person and the most capable of responding in a way that will be helpful and not harmful. I think that even in the most intimate human relationships detachment is a very important

thing, a very, very difficult but very important thing, because there is
such a human tendency to possess other people or to rely on them
in the wrong way: to live on their energy or to get involved in the
wrong way, to get into a symbiotic thing, which is not right. All
those things have to be thought about, and they have to be taken to
prayer.

One great blessing I think today is that people are much more
honest and forthright. They feel that they have a right to be themselves and not be frightened by what they find in themselves. I think
that candor and freedom from convention is good.

I feel more alive now in every way except physically; I can't do as
much as I used to do. I take delight in a lot of little things. It's a
healthy life. You feel real good after your chores are done. You feel
really like taking personal credit when your garden grows, even
though you had very little to do with it. I have even learned how to
make a little tent fire in the pouring rain, just enough to boil a pot of
water. I don't know why that fills me with such courageous satisfaction. It's such a ridiculous thing. You'd think I had cancelled all
wars. Every time I do it, I say, "Oh, boy!"

Sure, I'm afraid to die. My body is afraid, more of pain than of
death. I have days in me when I feel like I'm ninety-five years old
and there's nothing left in me, or what is left is senile and feeble.
That's just a bad day. But I also have days when I feel in me such a
desire for life, such a potential, such a feeling that there are all kinds
of unexplored things and all kinds of growing yet. You can't say
there is any objective basis for that. You can only speak out of your
own feelings, and I think that's precisely the difference between faith
and knowledge.

Just living up in the country, watching plants and animals live and
die, living close to nature, I've come to accept the fact that I'm not
going to figure everything out and that if I make a mistake God will
repair it somehow, or put it into context. Somehow it will become
part of something else. I have no idea how. I have no idea of what
God is like or anything, but I'm willing to take that on trust now. All
the messages that come to me as I'm older are reassuring along
those lines.

Death is like birth. If you were a fetus and all of a sudden something started bearing down on you and pushing you, you wouldn't
know what was happening. First of all, you are not very conscious
of human life; you're not a full human being. I would imagine that
birth would be a very unpleasant and frightening experience and
that life—well, just look at little babies. You know, life is just a glori-

ous surprise. I think perhaps death is very much like that, though. I don't want to play down its terrifying aspects. I don't think I could make a statement like that on intellectual grounds. I would be more inclined on that basis to agree with Sartre or Camus—that is, speaking strictly in intellectual terms, which is what they were doing.

But everything else about life contradicts that intellectual assessment. I would imagine that death is probably frightening and that it is sad, really sad, because you never live enough. I'd like to live about a thousand lives and be a different thing in each one. And all the things you regret, the things that cannot be undone, the missed opportunities, and all that. All the unfinished business, the leaving of people you love and all. There are no two ways about it: it's a downer.

But it wouldn't surprise me at all if it turned out to be simply like birth, being born. We don't know what the resurrection is, we simply know it is a transformation. If you believe that, it should take the edge. . . . You are going to experience all the fear and the terror and everything, but you are going to experience it in a context that isn't final. It is a question of belief rather than reason, and everything that I know about life now teaches me that *reason is very small* and perhaps one of the least trustworthy things of life.

I've been through a number of deaths and resurrections. When someone survives, I don't always know who it is. That's what it is—an identity crisis.

CHAPTER TWO:
RELATING

Just as I say my religious side has been underdeveloped, I feel in some people sexuality is undiscovered. I wasn't a virgin when I got married. I was very experienced. So I was in touch with myself sexually, and it was an important aspect of my life. There were times in my life when I really loved being a woman and loved being with a man. Dan and I never really had it together as well sexually as I have with other people. You can't have it all, and things did get better for us. We had pushed sex under the rug. I think we tend to overintellectualize everything, even sex. It is just an instinctual thing that you should be able to do, but our lives don't leave much room for instinct.

———Gloria Logan, Washington, D.C.

KATHY BAUMANN "My father wanted a feminine girl. Well, he didn't get her."

ANN FAREWELL "If you can survive relationships, you've got it made."

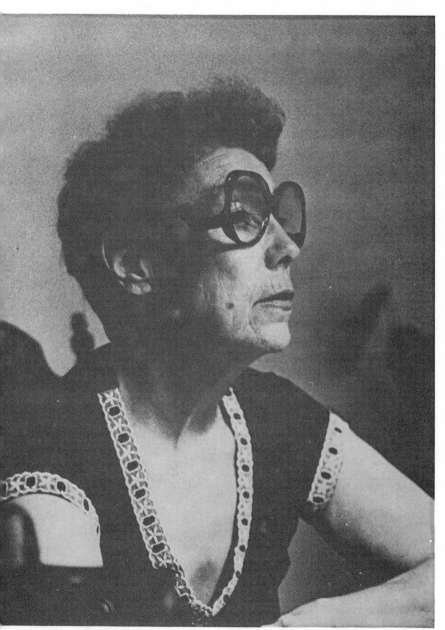
OLGA TORRES "I didn't understand an alcoholic, that it was a sickness."

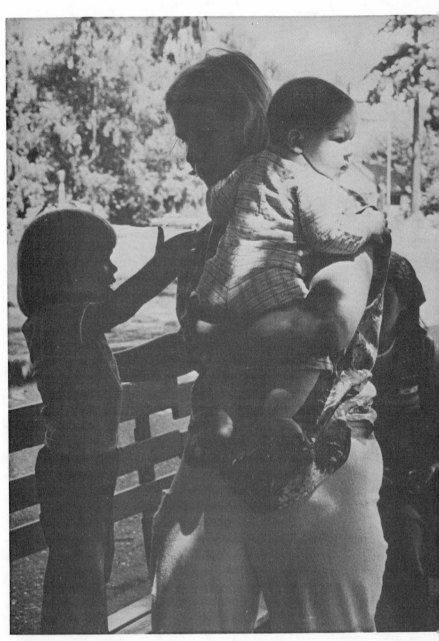

SUSAN DESCAMP "I really do see what happened when Christ related so to little children."

LINDA MARTIN "The first time I breast-fed was in the spring. It's like a prayer. Everything was budding."

JULIE HARKINS *(Boston, Massachusetts.) Occupation: Sister of St. Joseph. Age: 66.*

Question: Describe an instance in which you have given birth.

Answer: I think the most recent time . . . Well, in earlier times I have experienced giving birth when I saw a student begin living creatively and productively out of a conviction that I knew I had shared as a teacher. I think more recently, the times I have experienced giving birth would be when I have expressed something that has happened deep within me. I guess I have experienced recently being given birth to. When something that I have experienced very deeply within me, that I know is true, just absolutely meshes with something that another person has experienced.

Question: What is your relationship to other women?

Answer: I think I have good relationships with most other women. I have difficulty, though, with women that I experience as being harsh in a way that deals death. It doesn't matter whether the death-dealing is to me or to somebody else. I have a lot of anger with that sort of thing. Anyone who puts a pin in somebody else's balloon consistently tempts me to very uncooperative.

Question: Do you experience solidarity with women?

Answer: I think so. And a lot of pride. For instance, I saw my first woman policeman in town and I had to stop the car to say to her, "I didn't know we had a woman policeman, and I'm glad we do." She said, "Well, I've been a woman policeman for eight years." But she said, "Most of the time they kept me indoors." I have a lot of that kind of feeling. I often feel the desire to go over and say something to a woman because I just like the way she is or I find myself saying to somebody, a woman I'm passing in a department store or something, "You look absolutely gorgeous."

Question: What value do you see in celibacy?

Answer: I was secretary to the college theological society for a number of years, and the secretary and vice-president always had a lot to do with the national convention. I used to get very angry over the fact that the priests would always be over to one side and the women, sisters mostly, would all be on the other. I used to laugh because I never particularly felt that I was a great threat to anybody's chastity, but it was as if somehow they were attributing some kind of power to me, some kind of a danger. I thought that was sort of ridiculous, and felt I was losing some kind of valuable relationship that I longed to have. I certainly never had a desire to be in a world that was totally peopled by women.

I'm inclined to think that one of the real ministries of laypeople and of sisters is to priests. I think they are the most needy people in ministry, and that their training in relationships is terribly, terribly poor. They have been trained to be isolated, and then they have been literally sprung on people after a period of time. Priests need to be loved into being who they are and not be afraid. It's almost as if you have to hold out a piece of sugar to a very easily startled, very gentle doe and say, "All right, you can come near, I won't hurt you."

For me, celibacy is another phase of love. Love is not exhausted by married love. . . . It's another phase of love. It allows me to be a sister. It has opened up for me a much wider range of possibilities for friendship. You know, that took a lot of freeing through a lot of past experiences, and it has also opened up for me a whole area of co-creativity. I think of that when I think about giving birth. I'm posi tive that Father Nepper and I have given birth. Now, that's real co-creation. That's real man and woman. I am talking about the research we have done together, and spiritually, and intellectually.

I think that I had to fall in love and go through the pain first. I was in my mid-thirties when that happened to me. It is in the process of falling in love with a real person and facing the possibility of mar-riage that I came to recognize at a much deeper level of my being who I am and what it means to be a celibate person. It took me a long time to get over that, and my greatest regret is that we could not salvage the friendship. But I think it freed me for a future rela-tionship, so that now for the most part I feel very comfortable with men, and some men are among my best friends. Jerry Jeansonne, for example, is an intimate friend. I don't think that would have been possible for me if it hadn't been for the earlier experiences.

So celibacy is something to be desired. I am not restricted to hold absolutely precious one man and a few children, so I'm free to hold precious any number. And I do. And I love that. That is a very real phase of love. I am forced to admit that that preciousness I don't have, and it is a not-having, that is, a being without. It is just a differ-ent phase of love—not better, not worse, not higher, but just different.

Question: Do you cry?

Answer: I used to cry. I think I don't suffer as much now, either,
But I had this experience last November. I made a faith and community weekend, and in it we did one of those exercises where you
think back a little bit and do something with your geneology: who
are the people as far back as you can remember who were really
influential in your spiritual development? For the first time I put my
grandmother in it, and I couldn't figure out in that weekend why.

Two weeks later, I was mashing potatoes in the kitchen sink—and
I have never had one of those experiences where I see a succession
of images, though I've heard people talk about it. Of course one of
the reasons that I have never had anything like that is that I've been
such a head person for such a long time: many ideas and convictions and hopes and dreams and goals, but feelings? I've had a lot of
programming against feelings. When I first came to live like this in a
small community, I had some doubts about whether I might be a
human being still, meaning I didn't know whether I could feel constantly with people or live so close to others because I had lived
among such large numbers of people.

Anyhow, I saw as in a kaleidoscope these six faces, all women, all
sisters. Some of them I had experienced as being very resistant to
change. Superimposed on each of those six faces was the face of
my grandmother that I had put in my geneology for the first time. In
a flash of insight, I knew that I had never dealt with those six people
and that I was still very angry with my grandmother's harshness,
which she had never expressed towards me. I felt guilty about the
fact that I had been excluded from that.

I'm not heroic at all, or great about people who are harsh. I don't
trust myself, but I do trust God to only open a situation up if I am
able to deal with it. I may fall on my face, but I plan to learn how.
Maybe my grandmother, who is a woman, has been trying to talk to
me for a long time, but my heart wasn't ready. I was still too much
in my head. I believe that reconciliation is occurring. It is like the
line of the song, my favorite song right now: "The hopes and fears
of all the years of my grandmother and my mother are met in me."

That is reconciliation. I am learning that it is God who reconciles.
I am planning on being angry. You asked me about tears. Well, I
wept for my mother. In my family I never saw anger expressed. I
was born with that "never" seared into me. I was able for the first
time to admit that my mother was not a perfect mother. She's like
me, and in a sense, my sister. I remember that I had a lot fear, not

of my grandmother, but for her. I can remember the times we were alone when I was a child. I can remember standing at the sink while my grandmother washed me a stick of rhubarb and pulled off the rough. I can remember patting my mother's apron and putting my arms kind of around her knees and having that feeling of wanting to save her, but I didn't know what from. I don't think she wanted to be that way. That is probably where my anger came from. I hope in a few years I will be doing anger better. And more creatively. So, I am for life.

What is prayer? The old definition is the raising of the mind and the heart to God. Well, when does that happen? For me it happens in those moments like when I was standing at the kitchen sink mashing potatoes: that seeing and that knowing. God was offering that though my grandmother. That was a part of my salvation history occurring right there at the kitchen sink. Now, that's prayer. There is a joy and an enlightenment. And I'm not afraid.

KATHY BAUMANN

(Alpine, Wyoming.) Occupation: Former nurse; now owner of a small business near Jackson Hole; hunter; pilot of small planes. Age: 31.

Single.

I grew up in northeast Iowa. Majored in art at St. Catherine's in Minnesota. Studied nursing at the Mayo Clinic. Nursing was something I could get through, so I could make my own money instead of depending on my parents. Then I worked at the Mayo hospital for a couple of years as a school nurse. That was five years ago. We went through Jackson Hole on a school trip, and I loved the mountains and the people. When the trip was over, I packed up and moved out here in about three weeks. I packed my tent and my dogs, and was out here for good. I guess I'm impulsive.

I worked the slope trip here in the canyon as a driver for the white water trips, and in the winter I'd work the ski areas. Then I moved down here and got a house. I spend most of my time here at the gas station during the summer and go away during the winter months. I've done construction, cleaned motel rooms, worked in a bar and then a restaurant. I got this job from a guy who is my age. He wants to develop it into a city. I was looking for a good company to work with. I wanted the best. The company I found wouldn't let me be a boatman on the raft trips because I was a female. It bent those men all out of shape to have a female challenge them and be a whole lot better. I heard about this place and needed × amount of money to start it. I hired two young boys who didn't bring in as much as it cost me to hire them. Now I do it all. The one-man shop is the business downstairs and the apartment upstairs.

I live here. I'm the only one down here in this area that stays the night. I have a whole future here. I intend to be here a long time, because I intend to be part of this village as it is growing up.

Iowa people don't have what it takes to move on. I don't want to be sixty years old looking back, saying, "I should have done this, I should have done that, and I missed it." I didn't want to miss it. I want to live everything as fully as I can. A lot of people back home just sit around and bitch and complain because the world is giving them a crooked deal. These people I'm dealing with out here are extremely aggressive. If something is needed, it is done right now.

I work sixteen hours a day, seven days a week; I never close. But I only work six months out of the year. Everything we have is paid for before it is bought. This is not like the hospital, where there is always somebody telling you what to do. I was there so I could go on my coffee break on time. That is for the birds. So many of the nurses were there for so long it was just a job. The patient was something that had to be dealt with. So I got out. Now it's six months of work and six months of play.

I hunt in the fall. I got an elk last year, cleaned him, put him in the freezer, and I had my meat for the winter. I also enjoy flying planes. I'm a fighter too. I don't like to be walked over. That is why I don't fit in with the people in Iowa. I like being by myself. I like my dog. I like being with these people. I do keep my mouth shut more now and let people make mistakes.

When I am in close contact with people, I get tired of them. If I were to marry, it would probably be an arrangement where you go on separate vacations and have different businesses so you are not together all the time. I tend to find fault with people I'm with all the time. Sometimes I get sad and very lonely. I think basically I'm a happy person, though, happier than some who are not lonely but married. I want someone who is more aggressive than I am. Most people you meet today are hangers-on, and I don't like that. I feel suffocated.

I believe in God, but I don't feel that I have to go to church. The institutional church is not important to me anymore. I am hard on myself. If I'm not, who will be? I don't forgive myself too easily. I get angry with myself when I am weak because I don't like weak persons.

My generation has been described as lazy. I don't want to be a failure. I want to be wealthy. I enjoy working very much. I don't feel that I've opted out. I'm doing what I enjoy. I enjoy giving myself to other people. I get satisfaction out of it. I love to cook and give it away.

I am disillusioned with nursing, with marriage, with institutions, I guess. I want things now. I intend on being, not doing. I can't wait for a whole lot of change to happen.

I think if women are aggressive and intelligent, then they have something to offer. I look at a person as a person, whether male or female. When I offer something it should be taken, because what I offer is worthwhile. I have had men tell me I am too independent. I am not going to change so I can be marriageable. When the relationship is not based on the honest you, but on what you feel you should be, it can't work.

My father wanted a feminine girl. Well, he didn't get her. He always said, "You should do this or that, smell nice, look pretty, do nothing." I played football, ran track, had a tree house. That was not what I was supposed to do. I can look just as nice and smell just as nice as any other woman, but I can also be just as grubby and put down this cement floor when I want to and love it. It is what I enjoy. I want to know things—plumbing, building, everything. My parents had a hell of a time with me. Their way was unnatural to me. It was trying to be something I wasn't.

Now I'm delighted with the way things are. I couldn't ask for more. I have good friendships and working relationships with the people that are here with me. There is one fellow that is developing into an extremely good friend. It could be more, but I don't think that will be. It is becoming a fine friendship where there will be everything but marriage and sex involvement. It's based on business and one-to-one relating and liking each other. He gave me this business to get started.

I think children were the only thing for women for so long. That's all they were raised for, to have children and be in the home. That was what was most important to them. Then pretty soon the children grow up and leave. People are living longer, and so for twenty or thirty years this woman has nothing to do. In some cases women have to get out and work because families are so expensive. So the woman gets more aggressive, relationships change. I'm thirty years old. I've not been married, and I don't intend to be. It isn't that I have anything against it; I just haven't found that it fits into my life. It hasn't been the right place for me yet, I guess.

OLGA TORRES
(Las Vegas, New Mexico.) Age: 63. Spanish-Indian; one of thirteen children.

Divorced; mother of five.

I've lived in Las Vegas, New Mexico, most of my life. I was born there in 1916. Incidentally, I'm a Scorpio, so that is why I am so outspoken. I grew up in Las Vegas but I lived in Denver as a child with my stepfather. We came back to Las Vegas, and eventually he fell in love with some carnival woman and left us. Very poor, very, very poor. My mother had five at the time; she had thirteen altogether. My father was Swedish. I was one of the war babies. I was a Spanish-American War baby—no, really it was the first World War. On our side of the family we had the Juretas and the Bacas. They were all Spaniards, because the Spaniards settled around the territory of New Mexico. They came first without wives, and even though later on they went back and got their wives, they did mix with the Indians. My mother can't stand the idea of being an Indian. She says definitely there is no Indian blood in us, but she's never traced it back. Of course she's never tried. I never knew my father. I was born out of wedlock.

I was nineteen when I first got married. Not too young for around here. Many women get married around fifteen, and they start having their babies right away, which I did too. I had five children. I was married forever and ever and ever. My husband drank quite heavily, and I took some beatings that wouldn't quit. Every, every drunk I'd get beat up, and in between, kiss and make up. It was so great to kiss and make up, and then comes another baby. However, I was always protecting myself. I'd go to the doctor, and he'd say, "Well, we are going to put a diaphragm on you." But he didn't tell me that I was supposed to leave it in. So to go to the bathroom, I'd take it out. I think Gene is the diaphragm baby.

I had all of them all the way down—the pill baby, the rubber baby, the whole works. Then somebody says, "¡Cuidado! Watch yourself!" So I'm steady watching and praying the rosary because one of the priests told me, mind you, if you don't reach a climax with your husband, you can't get pregnant. So here I am, "Hail

Mary, full of grace," and he's working out like a champ, and I'm praying so I don't get in the mood. So anyway, that didn't work.

Well, the marriage broke up for the simple reason that my husband started drinking heavier and heavier, and then he got to that wine stage. He was a very good person when he didn't drink, but he was an alcoholic from a very young age. He was violent whenever he drank. If you didn't know him you would say, "Well, she's lying." He'd strike me so badly. Sometimes I'd be pregnant and here'd be my big old stomach and it wouldn't phase him at all. He'd kick me right in the stomach or something like that, and the next day he'd get down on his knees and he'd cry, and he would say that he'd blacked out completely.

I didn't understand that it was sickness. To me it was something they just used as a crutch. I'd condemn him for it, so half the time I was a bitchy wife. When he was sober, I'd bitch and bitch at him. He would bottle all this up, so when he did drink, I would really get it. I had no place to go. Here I was stuck with all these little kids, and it was a small town, you know; you don't want to make a scandal.

Then I started teaching school just with a high school diploma. It was during the war, and they needed teachers out in the rural areas badly. I taught for four years. He'd beg me not to work. He's the type that wanted to be the man. He was the macho. He had a job. That man always worked until the day he died. He had to go home and die.

You know, at first I thought I loved him, but I don't think I've ever known what love is, not even with a mother or father. My mother and I are pals, but she doesn't love me as a child. So I've never had that love, and not a husband's love. And with my children, I try to buy their love. I divorced my husband two years before he died, and so I try to make it up to the children by buying them things. My son Max had three cars when he was fifteen years old because I hit him one time and I felt sorry, so I bought him a car. It got wrecked up the second day, but something else happened, and poor little Max, I bought him another car. That's why poor little Max is the way he is today, I think. He is the one who drinks.

My husband was nine years older. He had been married three times before, and those three got beatings, too. I should have known better, but I was having such hard luck at home. I thought, "Well, this is a way out. I'll get married and I'll just get away from it all." I just wanted to get out of the house. My mother drank heavily

for a whole year at one time because my stepfather had just left her.
It was such a broken home that it was not something I wanted. My
mother would mistreat us. Her mother whipped her, and she'd whip
me, and in turn I'd whip my children. It just would be so cruel at
times. I hated being at home; I hated everybody there. Then my
aunt drank quite heavily, and I'd see this going on all the time, this
drunkenness . . . always its alcohol. It seemed like nobody could
have fun without it, and then there was fighting going around.

So I thought to myself I would get away and get married and have
my own house, and I wouldn't see this. I just thought it was kind of
nice to get married and be Mrs. I was always just "that girl," and I
wanted to be a "Mrs."—sounded great. You know, the more I think
about it, the more I think I should never have been married. I don't
enjoy being somebody's companion.

My husband's mother had English blood, and his father was
Spanish and Indian from Taos, but his mother and father were
killed in a buggy when the horses were frightened and ran away. So
he was raised in Colorado with some relatives. He had the high,
high cheek bones. Now, I don't know if you noticed Gene, but he
has the high cheek bones, and his nose is Indian, too.

Of all of my children I am close to Gene mostly, because he is
kind of the fatherly type. He takes care of mother. He is almost
overly protective, almost jealous of me. He doesn't want anybody to
hurt me. He is very sensitive. My daughter teaches in Santa Fe, and
my other son is a truck driver. I don't see him because his wife is
very jealous, even though I am his mother.

My son Max went into the service when he was eighteen, and
they stuck him in Adolf, Alaska, a God-forsaken place. There was
nothing to do there: no women, no nothing; and he was put in with
older men right off the bat. So since drinking was the thing, he
started drinking. There was a fight, and Max was involved. Someone in the fight got stabbed, and Max was blamed because he was
the newest and the youngest. He got court-martialled, and since he
was a Marine he got a bad-conduct discharge and went to Camp
Pendleton for a year. He didn't make it as the Marine he had
wanted to be. He didn't have much of a chance.

You know, I grew up with my children. We'd go dancing together,
all three boys. I'd come home exhausted from dancing the jitterbug,
tango, all these dances. I used to teach dancing. When I was young,
a troupe of dancers came to Las Vegas. One of the girls in the

troupe had an attack and left, so I said I would like to go with them. All I could dance then was the Charleston. Anyway, they taught me a few steps, and I could pick it up real fast. So off I went. I used to fill in for them. I traveled with them for about a year to all kinds of places: West Virginia, and all the Fox Theatres. That's where I learned Spanish dancing and castanet work. I was seventeen then.

When we went to Chicago we went to the Aragon Ballroom, where Wayne King played. And me from a small town, can you imagine? They always said there were floating clouds and stars there. Well, when I was there, there weren't any. I was dancing with this boy, and I looked up and this cloud started coming down and I screamed: "There they are!" Pointing up and screaming. He was so embarrassed being with me just then!

It was a good education, traveling alone. It was really great. And they took care of me because I was the youngest. It was really nice. I even started my own dancing school in Trinidad. I taught tapping, and my girlfriend taught toe dancing and ballet.

Then there was politics. I loved to be involved in politics. I dealt mostly with our people, I mean the Spanish people, in New Mexico. They don't really mean to sell their votes, but they figure if you're going to buy them on that day, you'll bring them something for it. It was one way to get them out of the house to vote; otherwise they wouldn't vote at all. You'd give them flour, maybe a sack of beans, maybe potatoes, and they'd vote the way you'd tell them. Even dead people voted. If they offered you coffee and you had to shoo flies away to see it, drink it. That's all they had to offer, and that's how you'd meet people. If you met the head of the family, his word was law, even if he was an old drunk. What he said goes; he was the main man, and that is how it was. For most of those people, that was all they would ever get from those politicians until it was time to vote again.

For me, the greatest fun there is is to dance. Does that sound silly? I *love* to dance. I don't drink or smoke because for some reason it makes me sick. I don't date too much, because those are important things to do on a date. Also, men sort of scare me. They always want to buy you a steak dinner and then go to bed. Well, first of all, I don't like steak. How about a hamburger or a bowl of chile? That's what I like. And why would I want to go for a car ride? Half the time I can drive the car better than they do. If I want a man, I want to have some say in it. I don't like them pushing me. Why am I supposed to really want that? Companionship? I've never found it, so I live alone. I *like* my freedom. I can go to bed when I feel like it. I can sleep when I feel like it; I can eat when I feel like it. I would rather be alone. This way, I figure, it's your house. If you don't like them, you can show them the elevator.

ANN FAREWELL *(Hamlin, West Virginia.) Occupation: Self-employed stained-glass artist; former "flower child." Age: 32. Education: B.A. in art.*

Divorced; single parent of two children.

I was married ten years. Two years ago I asked Bob to leave. I was pregnant when we got married. I was nineteen, a doomed statistic. I spent the first eighteen months of our marriage being pregnant; had two babies one after the other. Within three years or so, Bob was seeing other women. We adopted sort of an open marriage, which turned out to be very chauvinistic. I began to feel that we were immature and had never dealt with the basic problems in the marriage. We should have gotten counseling about our attitudes towards sex and my fear of getting pregnant again, but I think we just couldn't do it.

At the time we were living in California—in the days when everybody was supposed to be free and experience everything. We lived in Oakland in an expensive house and had a parade of thirteen or fourteen people through there in a year. I was trying to raise babies and be a full-time art student. Classes were disintegrating because they were tear-gassing Berkeley. I was still expected to be producing meals and cleaning house for all those people, none of whom seemed to have the standards I did. It was my home, and I wanted it to be orderly, I wanted to sit down on the couch and have some space that was mine. One of the boarders was a women's lib person. She went to all those meetings and stuff, and so we started having house meetings and tried to divide the work. The system worked until after she left. I was not a forceful enough person at that time to sustain it.

During those years when we were having housefuls in Berkeley, I tended to fall in love a lot, with everybody. The last time it happened, the person pointed out to me that I was married and there was no future in it for him. I had begun to feel that the whole thing was a symptom of something more basic. Bob was always in and out of jobs, and I sensed that his job instability was a kind of subversive method of declaring he really was not into the marriage, which had reached a point where it was destructive for both of us. I had always said to him and to myself, as well as to others, that if the relationship got that bad, it was silly for us to hang on, that it was time to get out of it. I hopefully all along felt that we would still be friends, but it didn't work out that way.

When Bob left, I spent about five months zonked out on the couch waiting for him to come back with flowers in his hands telling me he loved me. I had thrown him out, right? Well, that never happened. Utterly destroyed, he left and went to California to live with his parents, and he is rebuilding his life out there. We got together and talked over the phone off and on during that time period, and I realized he was feeling things I had felt six or eight months before. I could have empathy for him, and a real sadness that our feelings didn't coincide.

I can envision, now, living with another man, and I would very much like that. This whole question is really on my mind because so many of my friends seem to go directly from one relationship to another. It happened to me about three weeks after we split. I felt very attracted to a person. Love is just totally unreasonable. If it were reasonable, we would all be married to doctors and it would be a lot smoother and more ordered.

I was so intertwined with Bob that I felt like I was nothing. I got married so young that my personality was arranged around living with this other person, so it's taken me two years to figure out where I am. I have even had to rediscover what my own interests are. Very rarely when I was married to Bob did we have books in the house. Now I read all the time. I feel free to go ahead and do the things that I enjoy. It's just that somehow the energy got channeled into the wrong areas.

I discovered that a lot of things I was doing were a sort of reaction. A perfect example is cooking. I have just started *cooking*. I used to cook fine, but in the last couple of years of our marriage I began resenting being primarily the only person who was doing the cooking in the house. Bob was out of jobs enough so he could have gone a little bit in that direction. That just reminds me again of the ways we subtly get at people. Now, I do love to eat, and I do love to cook, and being with somebody who is an excellent cook made me get back my interest in it again. People are really good at putting fences up about recognizing things about themselves, and I think that is why counseling earlier on might have helped Bob and me. It takes a whole series of these circumstances to make you realize.

There was no real trust between Bob and me. It became obvious that we were on different tracks, and it would have taken years to repair that. I had a real sadness that our feelings didn't coincide. I guess what I am after now is a way in which a woman can respond to a situation, and how that differs from the way a man responds. A perfect example is by withholding sex. What are those everyday things that we not quite intentionally do to retaliate? I'm not sure a man does that particular thing. The thing I see functioning here is that I, who in the city was a very retiring person (I had only one good woman friend and no good men friends, and a lot of acquaintances), since moving here have established ties with people that I've maintained for six years now. They are close relationships that I have expanded far beyond the numbers of people I had known in the city. I realize I have undergone a personality change. Thirty years it took me to become the person I am, someone who functions in connection with other people. I think people are tribal, basically.

My mother and I were estranged for a long time because she didn't like Bob or the circumstances of our marriage. The last couple of years she has been out here. I think her experience since my dad died finally allowed her to reach some kind of understanding, and she has been real supportive. I am not living the kind of life she would like me to live, but she is accepting that. I think she realizes that I am happy now, and that is mainly what she wanted to know. I have no support system of relatives here, so she was worried about me for a while. But she is just amazing. It is ironic that it happened pretty much the year Bob and I split. Losing one relationship is painful, but at the same time I found myself repairing another. She waited until Bob was no longer on the scene, and at that time she chose to go ahead and be real supportive to me.

Given what he is doing now, and how we spent eight years living, I sometimes wonder if he didn't just become the most down-home and the raunchiest hippie of them all. I was hoping somewhere in there it would be too much for me, and I would throw up my hands in despair and say, "I'm moving on to something else because he has to live that lifestyle now." In one sense it was easier for me to move out here to these hills, without family and stuff, than it was for Bob, because he was always very close to his family, and they all lived near each other.

The idea to come out here pretty much started in California. I didn't particularly want to live in the suburbs because I thought it was artificial. I wanted either to live in the inner city and be involved in things or to get a place in the country, which I've always liked. But it was very hard to visualize Bob and myself earning enough income to buy land. I felt trapped economically. I was afraid that we would be channeled into a forty-year mortgage, and I said that there were already a good number of people doing that, and it was rather naive to count on our bodies holding together for that long. I just couldn't conceive of signing my life away. (It's starting to rain. Isn't it beautiful on the roof?).

We were two young people with babies dealing with people who were older than us. When we were first married, Bob was working for Penney's, and he was a brilliant young guy. He was going to spend the rest of his life working his way up in the company, and probably go somewhere because he was good at it. But then one of his managers who had been working for Penney's for twenty years was demoted in the department he was in, and that was pretty drastic for a man who had spent that many years of his life there.

As I said, the only people we knew were older than us. I hated going to parties where men used drinking as an excuse to start pawing you or making sexual jokes. It disgusted me. The women talked only about their babies and houses and the latest clothes, and I was not interested at all. Halfway through one steak dinner, Bob's boss started making innuendo jokes at me. I finally left the table. That superficial relating, and the use of stimulants as an excuse for horrible behavior, and just not relating to each other as people—the whole situation was depressing to me, the thought that I would spend the rest of my life doing this. Eventually we would buy a house in the suburbs and I would be Mrs. So-and-so. Then one day we walked through Haight-Ashbury as tourists and saw people in outlandish costumes having a really great time. Bob moved to that lifestyle first. I was still a nice suburban lady, getting up at 5:30 to put make-up on before going to classes. Eventually we traveled across the country four times in a flower van that never went more than forty miles an hour, and we ended up out here.

What I have learned most especially living here in the country and being in tune with the seasons and the cycles of life is that there is also death. I think this is different for everybody. For part of every cycle that is going on, there is a death of a relationship to that part. Everybody has different things they can move with and live with. We're born for various periods of time, and, for example, the problems of sexual craziness that some people have lived with in our generation are just not as important to those in another.

There are not too many women who live in this sort of a situation. Most have a support system: to be able to go down the street and see the same people every day and have some sort of context to put them in. I remember going to the supermarket and being ecstatic because there at the other end of the counter was a woman I had gone to high school with. She wasn't even particularly a good friend in high school, but just because I recognized her. I really feel you need to have some continuity around you.

I've never really been alone because I've got the kids, but being here without another person and without the children has been real good for me. It has given my life time—to read, to realize things that I would like to get done. I spend a winter here and grew closer to the children, which had not been happening with my marriage. I have a good relationship with the kids, and I am still here and making a living. Living with another person is a whole other movie that has to coincide with the things that you want to do and the energy that you would be putting into other things.

I have been more sure of what I have been doing in glass work. I enjoy doing that, and I have found a direction for marketing. I love my work, and I feel good about it. I am more sure of myself as a person, and it has taken me two years to figure that out alone. I like being alone in some respects. I am a very quiet person, and basically I spend my entire day here working and listening to music and working patiently at my glass work, which is very tedious. I do very intricate designs. I like being in the woods here; it gives me peace.

When I feel lonely now it is mostly because I would like to share the good things with somebody. I miss that. There are some things that occur during the day that I can come in bouncing high and tell the kids about it, but they do not respond the way an adult would. I call my friends and share it with them sometimes, but if I feel real lonely I end up crying. It's good to cry. I've been writing some poetry, too. It helps me get the images out. I've been feeling the need lately to play some music. I played the piano when I was a kid, and I've been plotting ways to get a piano up here.

I think a lot of people are really afraid of being alone, and the fact is we are born alone and we die alone. What I really feel is true is that the purpose for living is to grow in learning and love (it's really raining); and if through your relationships with people you are learning how to be a loving person, then that's the important thing. It ties in with the way you relate to people and the way you relate to the environment. People can make such a mess of it. If you can survive relationships, you've got it made.

GLORIA LOGAN *(Washington, D.C.) Occupation: Employed in consumer education for the Food and Drug Administration. Age: 31.*

Married; childless.

Where to begin? I decided to go back to get my master's in radio and TV, which was actually a very good thing. This is Credential Town, U.S.A. You can't have enough credentials in Washington. It's also the town for Ph.D.'s. Dan got a job on the Hill working for a senator. When I came here I wanted to get a job in television related to education. One positive thing I have to say about Washington is that I barely scratched the surface after eight months of job-hunting. You know yourself that in many other towns you would already have run out of places to look. You would have to take a job as a waitress. But here I knew that eventually something would happen.

Also, it was a period of recession. We were in a very difficult time, but we had high hopes in Carter and the governor of Illinois, who was a friend of ours. We just sort of thought a new spirit. . . . We came here knowing no one, no contacts, just picked up from Illinois when the administration was over, saying, "Where is the most likely spot for two people who both want careers?" My husband is a writer, and he got a job in four days: he just happened to find this young senator who was looking for a speech writer. So, really, it was because I had someone to support me that I could even take that luxury of waiting for something good to happen. There are thousands of secretaries waiting for something good to happen. I interviewed at CBS here, and they said (and I couldn't believe this) that they promote from within and their starting positions for women are secretarial. So after eight months of looking around and not knowing a soul, the way I got my job was through knowing somebody. It's who you know.

I'm with the FDA, trying to do some consumer education using the mass media and radio and TV. FDA has always been very industry-oriented, and we are trying now to get to the grass roots, thanks to the Carter administration. We want to get to the average consumer in the street. It's not just the FDA, but all agencies are seeing that public participation is going to be where it's at. Carter hired a lot of Nader's people and put them in cabinet positions. We have about fifty-five consumer affairs offices out in the field. That is what I really do here at the bureau level: develop support materials so that they can go out on the local level. One reason I'm glad I'm at the bureau is that a lot of our topics are today's, right in the news—food additives, the hair dye things, the nutritional labeling comes right out of our office.

We are involved directly with the Federal Trade Commission, so it's really sort of an exciting job. The nice thing about it is it's the first time I've done anything like this. As an ex-teacher who quit, feeling there must be more exciting things to do in life, I found out that all anybody wanted to know was how fast I could type.

I mean really, honest to God, I did not come up the easy way at all. In a way, I am part of the old guard. I see today young women coming right out of school and expecting a professional position. "I want a professional $50,000 a year . . . I want . . . " and I just get enraged. I sort of resent it. I used to look at older women and say, "Why don't they help us? Why should they resent what we want?" I think that is the big lesson that women have got to learn, to be friends and to help each other. Men always do that. Men cover each others' asses; they have the "old boy" network; they stick together. Women are somehow conditioned to be very catty, to feel that we've got to win a man, and it's me against all these other women. We're not a team. We are much more individual, which I could see as a strength. But the other thing is, some of the women I'm working with don't know how to handle themselves, how to be team players. They tend to want to go off in their own direction rather than looking at the whole, large picture. They get hung up on some small aspect, going crusading off on their own, and they refuse to be realistic about how the world operates. Then of course they are looked upon as men, and they make it hard for the rest of us.

I am trying to be nurturing to the young women in our office. We have one intern who is twenty-one years old. She is going on for her master's and Ph.D. She is ten years younger than I am, so she isn't someone I would naturally form an alliance with, but I really sort of go out of my way to get to know her, go to lunch, et cetera. Not that I am saying, "I want to teach you," but it is just sort of to be a sharing person. I haven't felt that much.

I'm feeling like this whole women's movement isn't going to make a hill of beans of difference. It has happened before in history—look at the suffragettes. It is involving so few women, and at a certain level I think we are making a lot of mistakes as women. We have totally told all these little women who are home having chilren that they don't count, that what they are doing doesn't have any status, any power. We have sort of alienated that whole group, and you just can't do that. If the women's movement makes any impact at all, it will be only because of simple economics. You've got two people working because of the economics today because women have had to go to work. They are going to want more money, and they are going to want to have more choices about what areas they get into. I really feel that the majority of women are not concerned with getting better jobs. Let's face it: they want to put a meal on their table.

Sometimes I have really good days: I like what I am doing, I think it's a good experience, and I am learning a lot. However, some days you feel like you are so ineffective, so buried under all these bureaucratic layers that to do anything you have to fill out forms in triplicate. It takes away all your creativity. You cannot be creative when you have to have something checked through seven different people and every little scientist is changing around the wording. Nobody has the guts to do anything interesting. One good idea is worth a lot of research to me, but this feeling that we need to do more studies is a real effort. I think that's one of the criticisms: more studies, more studies.

I didn't marry until I was twenty-six. The thing I found most attractive about my husband was the fact that he was the only man I ever met who had the same values as I do. We have a lot in common, and we are just really good friends. He never has bored me, even to this day. I could just spend days and days and hours and hours with him. We have a lot of time to think about ourselves, indulge ourselves.

The thing I am coming to grips with now is that I have been childfree. Pretty soon I have to face the fact that there won't be another chance for me; my options will be closed off and I will never have the opportunity to have this unique experience. Do I really want to be fifty and childless? You know, it is a whole different image when you are both in your fifties than it is when you are a nice young couple leading the good life (whatever that is). So we are trying to come to grips with thinking that whole thing through as well. I am predicting that there will be a baby about three years from now. Not a day goes by when I don't talk about it.

I can't make the conscious decision, but we practice birth control —and I'm telling you, it is getting harder and harder for me to put that diaphragm in. I'm thinking that after five years of marriage we have a better relationship than we had when we started. It would be nice to have a family. Dan said something interesting last week. He's a freelance writer, and he said if we have children he could stay home. I said, "Could you breast-feed them?" I don't want to be a superwoman. Today they expect women to be stimulating, pretty, educated, and have good careers and lovely children and da da da da da. If I decide to have children, I want to stay home for five years or whatever and enjoy them. My idea of having kids is not to work and then come home and take care of them. I think that is where economics play a large role in it today. I also think the women's movement is liberating men a lot. It is terrible the way men bear all the pressure.

Dan's a late bloomer. He's come a long way, and our whole relationship has come a long way, but that is because we both have given a lot to it, sort of nurtured each other at times. He is very supportive emotionally.

We are both lukewarm about religion. I call myself a lapsed Catholic, and the reason is that I feel you can never be an ex-Catholic. There is too much guilt. He is a lapsed Jew, which is a much harder thing to be, because for some reason Jews are really hard on themselves. I must say I haven't missed religion, but I have a feeling that when I have children I will. I am pretty sure that when we do have children they will be raised Jewish, because I think Judaism is so much more than a religion—it is a cultural heritage.

I said I don't miss religion, but in a way I really do. I didn't go to Catholic high school or college, so it was just my eighth-grade upbringing. My parents are religious, and they go by all the rules and regulations: they go to church every Sunday, my mother belongs to the Altar and Rosary, and my father is an usher. It is probably a whole side of my life that just has not been developed. If you don't play by the rules, you can't be involved. If you marry a Jew and if you practice birth control, you just cannot be a member of the club.

I studied music for ten years, and to me the arts and music are where it's at. I was an art teacher, and I get immense pleasure out of it. Music certainly gives me a religious feeling. Mozart is spiritual.

Just as I say my religious side has been underdeveloped, I feel in some people sexuality is undiscovered. I wasn't a virgin when I got married. I was very experienced. So I was in touch with myself sexually, and it was an important aspect of my life. There were times in my life when I really loved being a women and loved being with a man. Dan and I never really had it together as well sexually as I have with other people. You can't have it all, and things did get better for us. We had pushed sex under the rug. I think we tend to overintellectualize everything, even sex. It is just an instinctual thing that you should be able to do, but our lives don't leave much room for instinct.

SUSAN DESCAMP   *(Portland, Oregon.) Occupation: Administrator in an ecumenical, inter-denominational movement. Age: 34. Education: B.A. in social work.*

Married; two children.

My feeling is that women resent like hell the situations they were raised in, so they have thrown out the church and don't want any of it. Therefore it is just not part of many women's lives and spirituality.

Mary Beth Onk and I worked for CUE.She made a film on women in the church, and what she discovered is that women have a very low level there. Not just in the Catholic church, but in all established churches there is no place for women in leadership. There was a woman in the office next to us who had a theological degree, and she was a receptionist. At least the Catholic church has well-educated nuns, so they are ahead of other denominations.

The film was well done. It showed women getting the coffee out for a conference of male leaders, and growing up and seeing their mothers doing that as well at the Altar and Rosary societies and the Ladies' Aide and all of that. You accept it, I think,until you really start looking around at your world and at the things that make you angry about women's roles. The church is one of the worst.

I myself graduated from a Catholic college, where I had some really great theology and philosophy, very stimulating. Then I came home to the old family church in Portland. There was a couples' club and a teenage club, but nothing for my age group, the twenties bracket. Some of us talked to the priest about a discussion club, because a lot of us had come from some real stimulating situations. There were several colleges around here, and we wanted to get speakers, not just in theology—though that was where the big lack was because the Sunday sermons just weren't doing it. He didn't understand. He kept talking about ski parties.

I think there must be many women who are strong feminists and are part of the women's movement who feel this deep gap and who have found new relationships with women. There is no longer competition, or ladies in the corner talking about other women and diapers and stuff, but they are really excited about being good friends

with women. Yet the depth of a more spiritual base is just not coming out, for instance in places like *Ms.* magazine. What is coming
out, I think, is reinforcement for assertion and strength of character.
It's great for many women who didn't have a good self-image, but so
much of it is hung up on self, and just doesn't pan out.

When I got married, we surrounded ourselves with like-thinking
people, so we tended to think that everyone felt as we did. Just
after we married we moved in with two other families and bought a
house together. We three couples were exploring how to live a
church community in our own lives. Our jobs and outside activities
were associated with political and social change, and we wanted a
lifestyle to go along with that. We lived together for five years. The
community is still there, but we are not living with them. We were
able to part without terrific trauma, and we are still good friends.
Our community was child-oriented and built very much on the
strengths of the marriages. Our initial goal was to try to give to our
children. We were all raised in large Catholic families, and we
wanted to share with our children some of the good, positive inter-
action with other kids, dealing with adults and having loving relationships with them. We were ecology minded—with quantity cooking,
shared childrearing, shared material goods—so that we would have
more time and energy for other things.

It really did work. Much of the bond was our commitment, our
faith, and our involvement at the parish. It was in a poor neighborhood where they also had a free health clinic, a clothes closet, and
things like that. We are not a bunch of Jesus freaks. In fact, one of
our big struggles was trying to pray together, which we could never
quite come to do well, even with all our Catholic upbringing. Praying
spontaneously is the hardest thing for Catholics to do.

Mike got married when he'd been out of college for a couple
of years, and then he divorced. He learned a lot from that experience, and it helped us greatly, especially in the beginning when we
had a lot of tension and difficulty in communicating. I can see that
now he is a much more liberated man, even though his father is a
very traditional person and heavy into supporting the family and
being the dominating one. Mike has had trouble in trying to overcome that, especially now that we are nurturing little ones. We are
sharing it, and he doesn't have to take on all the worry. So living
together with others has really brought us all the sharing
relationships.

I majored in social work. I made the commitment to work for

others at the time (when you look back on where we were in the high school class of sixty-three). I still had the conflict between going to college and getting a nice little career or settling down with a husband. When I graduated from college, I looked around at most of my friends that were married or planning on marriage, and it didn't make sense. I was lucky. I got through that stage without finding a husband. When I first got out of school I volunteered for political campaigns for a while and lived at home and worked at my dad's business. I wasn't paid very much, but I never was a big consumer. There was an attitude in my family that supported the simple life and nonconsumerism. I was fortunate in my parents. They were also involved in the ecumenical movement.

What we have now in Portland is maybe a dozen women ministers or pastors, interdenominational, that for the most part are fascinating women, really fighting and generally getting into church and trying to get the church motivated to social action. Women are involved in planning here in laity leadership roles within the church, but I see that as unusual. Not many churches have brought in women as leaders.

The job that I have is part of an ecumenical, interdenominational movement in Oregon. There is a subtle block to getting up higher, into the real planning levels, and I don't know how to break through that. The establishment would rather have that "Father God" role in their bishop or the executive of their denomination, and a lot of denominations react adversely when a woman pastor arrives at their doorstep. I find it stimulating to be able to talk to women who are just realizing there is something here of real value to pursue and expand, and who want to get into the church organizations in whatever way possible. Often they don't see that they are qualified or have the ability to compete with men on the planning level. You can see that even in a woman who does tremendously valuable planning in her environment and is sixty years old: she still doesn't see she could do as well as males in decision-making.

The gates are open to a lot of women, especially if they think that they really could enter leadership. I do find that as soon as I start mixing with some of these church leaders I get very intimidated by their tremendous theological background and that sort of thing. But I also find that once I get into planning and thinking things through, I do okay. Even when they are not dropping names of books and things, I am constantly feeling uncertain in trying to realize for myself that I can do as well in the male arena.

It's hard to say without being trite that motherhood does do something for you. I am cautious here because I am heavy into little kids right now, but I really do see what happened when Christ related so to little children. They are so close to God, and their prayers are so simple and beautiful. When I hear my daughter's prayers it brings me up short. I stop being complicated and being spread too thin. It is simple and it is straight and it is a clear message to and from God. I know I am more tuned in because I bore this child and I have a high sensitivity to this child, and I see that right now as a huge contribution to the world.

The spirituality of living a Christ-like life is caring for others. I know you have to nurture your inner soul and spirituality and look to your own salvation, but you can't do that in a vacuum. I think the women's movement is doing a lot to bring together many of these areas that have been neglected for a long time. Everyone will benefit from women being happier with themselves as they discover room for more growth, more potential, and more of a future.

My husband is happier in our marriage because he does not have to bear the responsibility of a dependent wife and two children. This affects him psychologically and in his career. From my experience, shared responsibility has been a tremendous benefit in our marriage. The things that are being challenged are at the domineering level, but it is valueless to say that to someone in authority. Shared involvement does not sit well when we look at the conclave of bishops, where never except in an unusual situation does any woman have an influence, although that extra sensitivity that women have is needed in decision-making. It doesn't have to be a woman priest for decisions.

I don't want ordination for myself with the traditional role of the priest being the way it is. The theological nurturing kinds of things that we have at St. Andrews are what I'd like to see more involvement in. I know there are plenty of women who do want ordination. All the decision-making in the Catholic church has been done by the clergy, and that is the area I would like to see get penetrated by women.

CHAPTER THREE:
LIVING SIMPLY

"When my little girl was sick and dying from starvation, I was angry at the whole world. That man I was married to was sitting in the other room playing cards, and I was working in the fields to try to earn enough money to feed our children. I watched my little girl starve to death. I had thirteen pregnancies with that man in twelve years. And he came back to me after twenty-eight years of separation and divorce, and I took care of him until he died. When he found himself very, very sick, he remembered that when I left him, I had told him, 'If someday you really need me, look for me and I will help you.' He came, and for two years he was with me. He died right here on this couch, of cancer."

——Theresa Archuletta, New Mexico

THERESA ARCHULETTA "I live by the memories of my childhood."

MARY FELSMAN "The older I get, the more my faith becomes strong."

IDA MAE MORGAN

"In 1958 we hitchhiked up to Vashon
and bought up some old buildings."

"Saturdays we had to milk cows
and clean out places and feed
the hogs and shed corn."

"I got saved when I was seven."

"That morning at nine o'clock, we went down to the marrying preacher's house. It was a wonderful wedding, and so was the night."

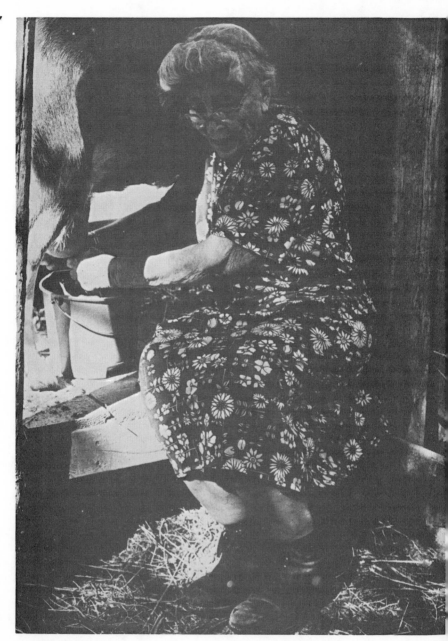

"And now I'm almost done milking these goats."

LINDA MARTIN "My dad is a carpenter and my mother grew up on a farm during the Depression, and they remember it."

JANET HURLOW "God has given me so many good and beautiful gifts."

GRANDMA STOLTZ "This trailer is where I sleep and eat, and I have all my sport in the garden."

THERESA ARCHULETTA

*(Albuquerque, New Mexico.)
Occupations: Campaigner for
second husband, a politician;
chambermaid in motels; worked
in Bernalillo County Mental
Health Center; forced to be on
welfare. Age: 59. Education: Two
years of college. Daughter of a
rancher and community judge;
one of fourteen children.*

*Married twice, divorced twice.
Six surviving children; four
adopted children; one child in
second marriage; raised eight
grandchildren.*

The world is full of whys, even the little world, because everything
the little ones see is adult size. When I was little, my dad was a
judge, and he used to say, "You wait your time and you will find
out. Sometimes you hurry too much." I know now not to ask too
many questions.

I was born in Red River, New Mexico. You can get there in a
truck, but you have to be a good driver. I'd drive anything, that's
the way we were raised. At the time when I was a young girl, you
know, people lived on very little: just what they could raise from the
fields where they planted. It was very rich land of itself.

My dad was not wealthy, but let's say well off. He had several
ranches; he had cows, he had sheep, he had goats, turkeys, rabbits,
pigs—anything you could look for, he had. He also irrigated the
ranch where he planted.

At that time we didn't know the difference between the day and
the night, our schedule was ruled by irrigating the land. We had a
day and a half to use the water, so I had to use it at night if it was
our turn. We didn't have any choice. If you put your water on, you
had to attend it. We had no machines in those days, but my dad
had lots of hands, that's what we used to call them, about twenty-
five. I was thirteen when I was the foreman and supervised them.

I was the fourth oldest. My oldest sisters were the cooks in the kitchen with my mother. I directed things with my father, and my sister helped. When he was away, I took over and he told me what to do. At that time it wasn't like it is now; no one said, "I'll tell you over and over until you learn it." I learned because I was ordered to learn. I started about three in the morning; it wasn't a matter of day or night, it was a life of twenty-four hours. Then, when I was old enough to go to school, I went maybe three months out of the nine because we had too much to do at home.

I remember at school one time the teacher said to me, "You wise kid. Are you the teacher or am I the teacher?" I stood up. I don't think I stood up because I wanted to be the teacher, but because I knew the teacher wasn't saying the truth to the rest of the kids. He said, "Never get in the water when you see it going fast." I said, "No, I am more afraid of the water that is standing still, because the running water can take me out of a deep place." He put me in the corner. I was angry. I told my grandpa.

I almost drowned one time when the water was very, very serious. No bumps, no nothing on the water, but I got pulled out by my braids. We went swimming in serious water and I could have been swallowed up. It was a whirlpool. I was warned by my dad always to be afraid of serious water. My dad found out, and I said nothing happened in the river. He said, "If you lie you go to hell." I said, "Hell is where we are."

My dad used to say, "We are all strangers. We are not brothers and sisters. But look, this world is made for all of us. So, you take people as they come. If they are mean, you deal with them fairly. If they are good, with more reason."

I live by the memories of my childhood. Let me put it this way: We were born and raised on a ranch. We knew what time the birds wake up in the morning; we knew what a snake could do and how you defend yourself against it. We knew when to cross a river and what were the signs of the river.

My dad used to take us out and we would do interesting things. He would teach us how to use a gun, and how to stay on a horse that was barely broken. (At that time there were wild horses.) By the time I was fourteen, I was already a cowgirl. I was a janitor at school when I was eleven, to help my dad pay taxes on his property. I used to get the wagon and the horses and go cut some wood. I'd bring it over and chop it for school and oil the floors, and sometimes teach if the teacher wasn't there—even if I didn't know much. But then, the teacher didn't either.

I thank God I lived with my mom and dad. My dad went to mass
a lot, but they didn't let little kids go. The ladies all had so many
kids. God lived with my parents. My father would get up early in the
morning. He would go to his desk and read there. Then he would
go outside and look up at the sky while we were sitting at the table.
He would always say, "Thank you, Lord. I don't know what this day
will bring, but I know that you will be there." Now that is the prayer
that I say every day when I get up. "Lord, I don't know what this
day will bring, but whatever I have to bear, you will help me bear it."

My dad could very easily see into the future. I remember in 1930
he decided to rent a huge lot from a rich man. And we started,
"Why, Why? Why plant more there when you have more than
enough here?" He said, "Because we are going to be in a depression
soon." To me it was all nonsense, but we did as we were told. He
made a fortune with what we planted. Then came a severe depression, and it went right by us; we weren't affected by it because he
was ready for it.

I married at the age of seventeen. I disobeyed my mother. She
said, "You marry this man, you won't get from me enough inheri-
tance to have even a chicken." He was a very poor man; that is
why she did not like him. I don't think I even loved him when I married him. He didn't do anything. I think I just wanted a way out, because when my father died I became the man of the house. This
man I married didn't even know how to work. I had to teach him
after we got married.

All that I liked of him was that he was very handsome. I assumed
that when I married him, since I could learn anything, he would
learn too. I went to work, and he stayed home. I got on a horse and
went down to see his mother and ask what was wrong with her son.
His family said he married me for my fortune. Little did they know I
was cut off. So I said, "I did not marry him to support him. Either
he does his share or to hell he goes." I took off on my horse and
went back and confronted him. He said, "I have my ways to make
the ladies love me." I went to talk to my mother. She said, "He is
your husband by law and before God. You will carry on even if it
kills you."

I did for twelve years. I had seven miscarriages out of thirteen
pregnancies with that man. He was a good lover, but that was all.
He never worked. I was pregnant all the time, and pregnant or not
I was in the fields working. The doctor said I couldn't carry them more
than three or four months if I kept working on some of those jobs,

but it was either that or starve. In Colorado I was pregnant and I was bleeding. The doctors told my husband to stay away from me, but he wouldn't listen. The doctors said I should divorce him because he still used me for sex, not only that but whatever way he wanted. He was the reason I was bleeding, because I was three and one-half months pregnant. He just wouldn't stop. He drank a lot.

I had trouble once when a priest asked me to sign a petition against abortion and birth control. I knew then I didn't believe in that petition, but I signed it. If I would have at least said, "I'd rather put a stop to me having children than seeing them go hungry and die, turning into a skeleton right in front of my eyes." There was no birth control in those days; the religion was against it. If you married, you were to have all the children you were supposed to have. I used to tell my mother, "Why should I have to make the whole world myself?" I was nothing but skin and bones, and still having and having children. "Either you come and serve me or I will make you!" That was the life then. There was only that—just: "Hey, come! I need you." My mother told me that when I marry it is forever, but I couldn't stay with him.

It was a matter of starving or work for me. I had six kids, but Annabelle died of hunger and my hands were tied. I was working for two dollars a day to support my husband and children. My family never wanted to give me a hand. They cared for their ranch hands, good care. When you disobey, you pay the price.

When my little girl was dying the doctors said she was not really sick; I was to just give her things to eat and she would be all right. I was angry at the whole world. The man I was married to was sitting in the other room playing cards, and I was shoveling snow just to be able to get out of the house. I watched my infant girl starve. After that I divorced that man.

He came to me twenty-eight years later when he found himself very, very sick. He remembered that when I left him, I told him, "If someday you really need me, look for me and I will help you." So he came to me and he died with me after years of separation and divorce. For two years he was with me, and the doctor came and gave him morphine shots. He died right there on this couch, of cancer.

Lately many things have happened to me that I can't explain. I hear voices, and I see visions. I read the psalms and I hear a voice. I feel a chill like somebody is there. I lie down and I pray the rosary. I say to God, "Where are you when I need you? I live for you, I eat with you, I drink with you."

Not long ago I had to quit my job as a chambermaid in motels. I went to the hospital for surgery. I had a malignant tumor, and there was such pain. I was lying there and I heard someone say, "Give me your hand." I was afraid, but I gave my hand. I began to move. I was telling the man who was holding my head not to press too hard. It didn't dawn on me that he couldn't have been the one also holding my hand, since both of his hands were on my head. It was like going through a tunnel. I was healed. The doctors couldn't believe it. I said I had a lot of people praying for me. I had faith. Look at me now. I haven't got any headaches and I walk straight now. I will never give up. This world will go to hell before I ever give up.

MARY FELSMAN   *(St. Ignatius Indian Reservation, Montana.)*
Occupation: Housewife.

Married three times; widowed twice; gave birth to four children, raised two and lost two.

People are all different wherever you go.

When I was about two years old, something happened to me that caused my hip to be misplaced, and it has been like that ever since. Sometimes things happen that can make one bitter. At that time, my folks were poor, and my mother was just a little bit educated. She only went as far as the third grade with the first sisters that came here. So anyway, I felt that I was different on account of that misfortune that happened in my life. My mother never brought it up. Of course I never asked her really what happened. I just kind of kept it to myself.

I didn't realize I was crippled so much, but that didn't mean other people didn't notice, especially as I grew older. My aunt told me there were two stories on how it happened. One was that I fell off a stack of trunks, and my mother didn't know any better, so she just left me that way and I eventually learned to walk again on a misplaced hip. The other story was I fell out of a rope swing we had. My dad and mother told me that in those days there were no doctors, but I still blame them. They could have done something. It made a lot of difference in my life, but I still went on doing what other people did. I would ride horses, all right.

My mother didn't ever bring us to a doctor. She called on this man and he came over and doctored us. He sang medicine songs, and then he asked a blessing. He talked to the spirits. Then he touched you—your head, your body—and then you got better. My mother also had certain roots that she boiled and gave us. She was the one who made the medicine for coughs and colds.

When I was very, very young, we used to go on hunting trips in the fall to gather our meat supply, and we would ride the horses over the mountain trails. I remember very little about it, but one year there was so much snow and we were coming home over the mountain. We had one husky man in our tribe who was very strong.

We called him Buck Finley. He'd break trail because the horses would get too tired in the deep snow. I was in the back with my mother, and she would be guiding the horse. When we got to camp there would be so much snow we could hardly make camp. Mother and father went to get poles to put up the teepee, and they set me down under a big tree. I was so cold while I waited, and my leg hurt a lot. When the teepee was up, we put blankets in it and had a fire. The snow was so deep and cold, and we were right on top of it. We stayed there the whole night and I still had my mocassins on. In the morning my mocassins were all shriveled up because I had put my feet in the ashes during the night to keep warm. I cried a lot. I remember that. Finally my mother told me I couldn't go on these trips anymore because they were too hard on me, so they put me in school with the sisters when my mother and my father went to gather meat in the fall.

My mother did all the work on those trips. She gathered all the wood, besides taking care of the meat. It would be all stacked up and she'd have to slice it. She would make little racks in the teepee, up above the smoke. That way we'd smoke the meat and dry it at the same time. She would dry one batch of meat and then store it in big squares of rawhide. Then my mother would tan the hide, take the hair off it, and scrape and partially dry it so she could take it home, where she would finish working on it. Then they made all those mocassins from it.

My mother never lived with me after I became a woman. She never liked my corner here; too noisy with people all around. They have moved in, almost touching your house here. She lived out by herself near a stream in the mountains, and she liked it that way. One time she got sick and I found her at home. She agreed to come home here with me for one week, so she must have been pretty sick. Then she said she had to go home where my father left her when he died. Towards the end she had broken her hip, so she used a walker. She insisted on taking care of herself. She told me, "Don't you ever give up and want people to wait on you and take care of you." She was ninety-five when she died.

My mother and I were part of the old-fashioned ways. We talked, but she didn't tell me things. I had to learn that later on, on my own. She only told me, naturally, to be afraid and not to get involved with men. She told me that, but she didn't tell me too much about sex and all. You're not supposed to know! She was against me marrying, ever. That was bad enough, that she told me that.

She told me I was not like other girls, because I have a bad leg. She said she wanted to keep me home with her always. But I did get married.

My mother wouldn't accept the man that came to ask for me, who I later married. My brother helped me to get a license. I was only seventeen and he vouched for me, saying I was eighteen. My marriage wasn't set up, that was done before my time. I think my brothers and sisters picked who they married. I have an older brother, and he was younger than his wife. Of course, he was the son and could do pretty much what he wanted to do. I think it was much easier on the boys.

I made out all right, even with my bad hip. In my first marriage I had four children. I only raised two: I lost one at birth and one at a year and four months. My oldest one and youngest one I raised. As far as my married life goes, well, my mother always told me you have to be faithful and all, no matter how hard it is. Then my husband died.

I was married again after that, but I didn't have any more children. I don't know why; I didn't use anything to prevent it. Of course I was older. My second husband died of a heart attack. Henry here is my third husband, and I've only been married to him for fifteen years. I would say God put us together. His wife died and he was alone. He was just a lonely little man, and I was alone at the time. We are fine companions. We knew each other all our lives. We made our first holy communion together, and we got confirmed at the same time. I know God put us together. I have no thoughts about making changes. I just took things as they come, and I still do. I had some beautiful daughters. My second daughter died of too much medication for arthritis. She was bleeding.

I had the very sorrowful experience of losing my two little brothers in accidents. That's when my religion kind of went against me. I can't believe that one of them went to hell. We don't know what happened, but he was drinking and his truck ran over him. They say if you're drunk and you die, you go to hell, but I just don't think he went to hell.

Then I had another brother who got killed on the highway. Somebody had taken his car, and he was walking in darkness. He had a beer in his pocket that he was taking home when he got hit. The first car didn't kill him. They put flares up, but then the second car came and hit and killed him. That's the only time I doubt my religion. I went to the inquest. Just because they found beer in his pocket, they tried to make it look like he was drunk. This lady that hit him first, she said he was alive and she begged them to take him off the highway. You know the rule: you're not supposed to touch anybody that was hit. So they left him there and the second car came. With the flares out, they still ran over him. That was too hard for me to take, and I doubted my faith. He had seven children.

I just think we have to suffer. It happens. The older I get, the more my faith becomes strong. I have had a hard life, I would say. It wasn't easy, not at all. But I have had a lot of blessings. I'll never forget this one blessing. I was going in the early morning to pick up this lady's wash that I was helping out. I was just singing in a happy early morning. A car came straight for me, and we collided. There was nothing left of my car, but I was blessed: I wasn't hurt at all except for some glass.

More blessings are my great-grandchildren. I live for them. We took care of one, Eileen. We had to potty-train her and so on. She's our favorite, Henry's and mine. I've also had a friend all my life, the same one, a white lady. When I was twelve she came to play with me. My mother and I were digging roots and she asked what we were doing. She is still my very best friend. When I lost my second husband, she came and stayed with me. When my car broke down, she went over there with me to get my car. I mean, when anything big happens in my life, she is there. I have other friends, too. When my sister and my mother died, so many showed up. Then you find out, in time of need. Then you have friends.

IDA MAE MORGAN *Vashon Island, Washington.*
Occupation: Missionary to Indians; tends
goats; makes quilts.
Age: "Over 78."
Daughter of a horsetrader.

Married, with four of five children
surviving.

I can hardly walk. Two-hundred-fifty dollar shoes! The first pair are
out on the porch. Thank God my feet don't go. These over here are
my tourist shoes. I had them about a year and there was a crack,
so I took them back. The man said he'd never seen anybody wear
out shoes like that, and he'd been making shoes for forty or fifty
years. Well, my daughter said to him, "Bet you never saw anybody
who'd work on her feet eighteen to twenty hours a day, did you?"

I'm over seventy-eight. I did work for more than eighteen to
twenty hours yesterday. I make and sell quilts for the Indians.
Sometimes when I get a chance I send them down to a mission in
Arizona, a little way from Phoenix. I taught there one year, and
another year I cooked. There were 180 students at that school. It's
been over twenty years since we helped to start one eighteen miles
this side of Albuquerque. My husband, Floyd, helped on the
buildings. I have pictures of him there working on the buildings,
remodeling, getting ready for the classrooms. So we are interested
in that school. Some of the neighbors here got interested too. They
never knew what was going on in the Indian reservations. We've
had quite an influence on other people.

I think I have been a missionary all my life. I got saved when I was
seven years old, and the Lord wonderfully saved me. I was the third
child. I had an older brother and sister. We walked about three miles
to school, and there was a meeting going on. People were getting
saved, you know, and I said, "I want to give my heart to Jesus." My
brother and sister said, "Oh, you don't know what you're doing." I
said, "Yes, I do. I want to be a Christian and give my heart to
Jesus." They said, "You will be afraid," and I said, "No I won't."

So that night, sure enough, when the preacher preached—I tell you, if I was one hundred years old and had lived in sin all my life, I couldn't have felt any more wicked than I did that night. I stood there, and the tears ran down on the desk and on the floor. An old lady came along, who was praying with different ones. When she got to me, she said, "This little thing doesn't know what she's doing," and then went on and prayed with some other people. My heart was just broken because Jesus came in and saved me with such peace and joy that I said within myself, "When I get to be a big woman, I'm going to tell all those boys and girls that Jesus can love them and save them." That was in 1907.

The Lord called me to be a missionary when I was ten years old. I would just cry and cry at night, and my parents would say, "Ida Mae, you just have to go to sleep and stop that crying." I was crying because I thought I was going to be a missionary and go across the ocean, and I was afraid of water. I didn't realize you couldn't just be a missionary. Nothing ever opened up.

Then I got acquainted with this boy—well, I'd been acquainted with him all my life. When I was eight years old, we came about nine miles to the schoolhouse to have a potluck dinner and a morning service. After we had eaten our dinner, here came an old surrey pulled by mules, and some old folks got out. An old lady (well, she wasn't old, but she was to me) got out and was sitting in the shade of the tree. She said, "You know why we didn't come to meeting this morning or to the potluck? Well, my oldest son. . . ." Then she told about her oldest son, who was staying with somebody. They had waited so that they could come all together. She began to tell about the boy. He was so kind and so patient, and he took care of his little sister and was nice to his brothers. He never fussed with them. I was a playing around, you know, and I thought, "If I could see that boy." Now I was only eight, but I had lots of brothers and sisters. An uncle lived with us, and a cousin. Well, they were little snipes as far as I was concerned; those boys were nothing.

So as I grew up I wanted to see that boy, but he lived in another county. My daddy was a horsetrader, and he'd go down into that other county and pick horses and trade them off. I would always want to go ride the horse or else go in the buggy and then drive the horses back. Now, I wasn't half as anxious to go see about those horses as I was to see where that wonderful boy lived, down in western Kansas. He is four years older than I; he was twelve. It was

love before first sight. He was a cowboy and didn't even go to
church. It was a burden. I thought I would die if he didn't get saved,
but I didn't tell anybody. I didn't talk to him, because there wasn't
an occasion. Then I went to high school about twenty miles from
where he was going to live. I was praying for that Morgan boy;
every time we went to prayer meetings I just prayed that would be
the night he would be saved.

Saturdays we had to work awfully hard at home. We had to milk
cows and clean out places and feed the hogs and shed corn. I was
still praying for him all that time. Sunday we had to go down to the
schoolhouse where we had a little Sunday school. We hurried and
fixed a little bit of lunch. We got cow chips and put them in the
stove quickly so that we could hurry. By that time pappa was ready,
and we sat in the back of the wagon. I can remember my feet
hanging out, and we were singing. I was the happiest girl.

Then one Sunday I just knew what the Lord had done; I knew
that Morgan boy was saved. So we drove down, and when we got
pretty near, a friend ran out and she said, "Oh, Ida Mae. that boy
got saved." We married a couple of years after that. I wanted to
make sure that he was the right one.

He was pretty well fixed for a young fellow when we got married,
but he had to go into the army right afterwards. We got married on
the ninth of June. We were busy and we had to work real hard, and
he hadn't come up to see me for two weeks before we were
married. He finally came up the Saturday night before. I had to help
make five cakes and dress nine chickens and milk thirteen cows the
day before I got married. When I went to make the beds, I wanted
to see if he had a new suit. I opened his suitcase, and he had his old
grey suit, but he had had it cleaned. It was all folded in the suitcase,
and that was what we were supposed to get married in.

That morning at nine o'clock, we went down to the preacher's
house, the marrying preacher down about nine miles. It was a
wonderful wedding, and so was the night. Then the next morning
we went over to help with the stock. A man came by to pick us up,
and the car was so full I had to ride on his lap. When I got over
there they said, "If your mother knew you were sitting on Floyd's
lap, she'd have a spell." And I said, "Well, can't I sit on my
husband's lap?"

Well, we went down to his place, and on Wednesday we got a
letter saying he had to go into the army. But we had a friend who
said he would go in Floyd's place for a month, and they let him do

that. So we stayed home and got the crop cultivated. Then he had to go.

Next came those terrible winters where the snow would be in drifts as high as the windmill platform. Stock just died like flies, and everybody lost. In the spring, why, we'd go out to skin the cattle, because we had lost our cows. I'd go out and skin ninety head of cattle, and I was pregnant. The snow was so deep we'd pull oil cake out on the sled and put it in piles for the cattle to eat, because they couldn't eat the grass.

I had five children. The first one died, though, I think because of the life that we had to live. Floyd took me to the nice home that he had filed out in Colorado. It was a dugout thirteen by thirteen, with dirt steps and a dirt floor and dirt walls tinked with mud, and over the top were boards. We didn't have much to eat. Where we went to get water, they had a quarter-mile row of winter onions, so we had creamed onions and fried onions. We still do like onions.

They didn't have a Sunday school, so we started one in what they called Blaine. We went over there, about eight miles I believe, in the horse and buggy, and it was cold, you know. We had three children at that time, so we'd put a wagon sheet down in the front and then the featherbed, and then put the babies on that. We'd go to the schoolhouse and get the fire going, and they wouldn't come in until they saw the smoke. Our work would start with the children.

The Lord laid it on our hearts about the Indians when we were in Seattle. We had started a church in Oregon, and the Lord spoke to us there. Well, I thought I was having a dream, so I turned over. The Lord said, "I want you to go to Seattle and start a Sunday school a mile and a quarter southeast of the Japanese gardens." Well, I had never been to Seattle in all my life, and Floyd said everything was blacked out in Seattle and he didn't think it'd be wise to go up there. Anyway, we didn't go. We bought a home and fixed it up. It was right near the veterans' hospital, and I was a nurse. We moved so many times, and nothing ever opened up.

One day I got a phone call from somebody up in Seattle, and he said, "Mrs. Morgan, I know you want to start a Sunday school in Seattle, and I have a building located here. You'll have to be here before Thursday because they are going to have a meeting to dispose of it." I called Floyd long-distance; he was out in Oregon picking pears. And he said, "Yes, but mama, you'll have to give up your home if you do that." So I said, "If this is the Lord, I'll do it." So he came right home and we loaded up the trailer and car full with stuff.

We drove right up to the place in Seattle, and I went across the street and knocked. A lady came out, and I said, "Can you tell me where there are any Japanese gardens?" She said, "You are about a mile and a quarter from them now," and I said, "Thank you." I went back to the car and said, "Daddy, this is the place; unload."

So we did. There was an old straw building with a parsonage in the rear. I wish you'd seen that parsonage. It was an old streetcar that had been used for a chicken house. There weren't any windows, and you could have thrown a cat through the crack. I measured the chicken manure in there, and it was eighteen inches deep. Well, that was where we started our Sunday school. We pastored there for nineteen years and built a nice home. I nursed in the daytime, and sometimes at night too. When I got home one evening, I said to my husband, "You know, I think we ought to build a church." I don't know how we ever got all those buildings done. The Lord just worked out one thing and then another.

Floyd was never a farmer. He didn't like the farm, and I thought when we moved out of this place he would just forget about it. He has been a marvelous man. He has never said a cross word to me in all these years, and we've been married sixty years now. He was a real cowboy in western Kansas and Oklahoma and Texas. We still love each other all the time. We'll have people at the table, and sometimes he'll pat me and I'll pat him. But he has been sick. He's not able to—well. . . . he is one dying man, darn! Of course, he is the best man I ever had, the only one. But you know, he is so kind and so patient and long-suffering. I guess he had to be to put up with me.

In fifty-eight we hitchhiked up to Vaschon and bought up some old buildings and fixed them up, and then we got some more lumber and I put this house together. We started a Sunday school. Two of my oldest children passed away, and one is a Methodist minister. He's been preaching for thirty-one years. A good life, a good marriage, never a cross word. You have to have a Christian marriage to survive it. I really think it is the only way, for a good marriage anyway.

There now, I'm almost done with milking these goats. You have to leave some of the milk in or it'll dry them up. This goat doesn't like Floyd because he's got britches on, and anyone that has britches on they don't like. That one over there we raised in the house, and so she is housebroken. I used to let her play out on the lawn, and then she would go in and do her job in the box. These chickens over here, this one is getting ready to lay.

I preached for years. I fill in now only when the preacher's not there. I love the goats. I like to supply people that are sick with milk. I like to do anything where I think I am helping somebody else. In church this morning when they wanted somebody to give testimony, I got up and said, "The Lord has been so precious to me lately." I said, "You all know that I make quilts. I put them down on the floor to pack them, and I have a blessed time with the Lord praying for the Indians and the missionary work while I'm quilting. Everything I do is for the Lord, but some is double."

JANET HURLOW   *Mt. Pleasant, West Virginia.*
Occupation: Housewife; author of Psalms
from the Hills of West Virginia *(Bear & Co.,*
1980).
Education: "Very little."

Married; mother of four children.

To me God is not a judge, but very beautiful. A kind and loving
God, very gentle. He is colorful, and he has personality. He is a fun-
loving God. He just doesn't sit up there all the time and say, "I am
gonna get you and you and you." I mean, you know, he smiles, he
laughs, and he plays. He's a very active god.

I experience God everywhere. He lives with me from the time I
wake up until the time I go to sleep. Of course, God lives more in
the church, but he lives with us. He is in everything, in all the
beauty of nature. I believe that God is within us. Of course, I've
been told that his kingdom is here on this earth, among his people,
and I believe that, too. In fact, we were discussing this at Vienna,
talking about Jesus coming back, and I said, "I don't see why Jesus
has to come back, because Jesus is already here."

Vienna is where the Religious Institute is. I went there to learn
more about my church, because I'm a Christian teacher at the
church, and I went because once in a while I like to get away from
my family a little bit like that, not too long. I think of them all the
time, because I love my family. When I come back home I appreci-
ate my family more. I can stay in the house all the time, and when
something needs to be done it just passes me by. But if I get away a
little bit I can see it when I come back.

Maybe I get a little grouchy with my family at home or something
like that, and I have time to think those things out when I get away.
When I come back I think I'll be a little more kind to my family. I'll
tolerate them a little bit more; I'll change in these little things. And
usually it'll work out that way. Then I like to go back and cook and
clean and just live a simple life. That's the way I am. I'm very lucky
with my family.

My father and mother were divorced. I don't believe people
should get divorced and marry again, but I feel like my mother and

father could never have done anything wrong. When my father brings his second wife to my house I treat her kindly because she is another human being and everything. She's a nice woman, and I like her. I would never put anybody out of my home and use the excuse I was a Christian acting in the name of God or anything like that. I would not do that. And I realize there's just lots of divorce. We have had our trouble in our family, but we've been able to work things out. I feel like anybody could work things out if they'd just try. Divorce is too easy nowadays. It's just an escape. I can't do anything about divorce, abortion, and hunger in the world, people's going hungry and things like that. I just pray.

I worry about my kids when they get big. There are some things in this day and age I would like changed, but of course I can't. But I realize my children have already gone out into the world. I think that maybe they will try those things or something, but I take them into church and teach them about God. I realize my children have more of a chance than most do. Like their cousins — they've never been taken to church. They might fall into these traps that we have in this day and age, like dope and alcoholism. All this stuff, there is more of it than there used to be. It's hard to understand.

It's only natural to worry. There was a time we were very poor, but of all the problems I've had, God has brought me through them. Even sometimes when my family has been hungry, people would bring things right to the door. We had a neighbor (he's dead now), and when my family was going hungry he used to go out and get game and bring it for us to eat. Of course the neighbor didn't know that we were hungry or anything like that, but I felt like that was God feeding my family directly. Anything we have needed, all I had to do was ask and God would provide it for us. We wouldn't be alive today if it hadn't been for God just giving us things we need, sometimes indirectly and sometimes directly. We would ask, and maybe in a few hours or something there would be just what we could use, right at the door.

My husband is a good guy. He came into the church. He goes to mass and everything, and he even got a better job. About the only worries I think I have now are other people and the condition of the world and all that. As far as my family is concerned, I have a very, very good family. My husband works construction now, and we have enough. We don't go hungry anymore, and if the kids need shoes and clothes, we can get those things. I can get around, like I said, and we can go places. Since I began to write these books, my whole life has changed. There was a time when I was a sad person, I didn't get involved in things like I do now. I think I'm really on my way to becoming the person I'm supposed to be. I'm really satisfied with that.

I don't know why God chose me to be the one to write this message now. Like I said, I'm not a person to write. I don't have the education. But like it says in the Book, some of these things will be given to the poor and the lowly people. I think God has given me a beautiful gift. I can't describe exactly how or why. I do know that he said it was for other people, that's all. I can say that when he gave me a gift I was supposed to share it with everybody in the world.

I'm just an ordinary person, like everybody else. Just because God decides to give somebody something doesn't mean they're really holy or anything like that. He could give it to anybody he gets a desire to give it to: he could give a gift to you, or to the president of the United States, or anyone. Anybody he decides to give a gift to, he gives it to them, regardless of who they are or what they do. They just have to be open to it. But like I said before, the person that writes has to be a person that scrubs the floor and digs in the earth and does all those little things. They have to be a small person; they can't think they are better than anybody else.

God has given me so many very good and beautiful gifts. My husband and my children. As anybody can see, they're strong and healthy and talented and beautiful. My whole family is, in fact. When Lisa was born, she weighed four pounds and nine ounces. She was so tiny. And I went to sleep and dreamed that sometimes the tiniest things are the most precious. I looked out, and there were two little white butterflies fluttering there past the window, and I thought, "Well, that must be a message from God." That was the gift from God, Lisa.

Why, God even gave me the church. Even that was a gift. I couldn't find the church, and God just reached down and picked me up and gave it to me. When I was a child, I lived back in the country, and I didn't know about the modern world. I lived on a farm with my grandparents, and we came to town about once a year. Way back then, maybe once a year I would go to the Protestant church way out in the country, so I didn't know anything about the church. When things would bother me, I would just go out among the trees and everything, and maybe watch the water or just sit someplace where it was green and beautiful and walk through the field and get away from all the problems I had in the house. I feel that God spoke to me through those things.

Maybe a few people can still go back to the land, but there's not enough land left for the people. All the cities that are being built, and all the plants. And there's television and there's running water and there's electricity and all of these things that people would have to leave. These are or have become a necessity of life. When you really go back to the land, you leave those things behind, and you work. You work in the soil and you raise the animals. There are so many people used to the city life, and they could never survive. They wouldn't know how. There are probably lots of people that wouldn't like to go back to the land anyway.

It's natural for people to want to be close to the land. I never realized that there were people that didn't do the things I do, like working in the house without any shoes on, people that don't have a good time and enjoy their life. I feel like we can have all the things we need, plenty to eat and everything, and not get so keyed up with things. Like what they tell you on television is all prefabricated, people always having all these worries and things. I mean, they don't live a rich, full life like we do; it's just story, made up. And all that worry about clothes—some people wouldn't even let their kids go out and play in a mud hole! I think children like to get out and splash around in the rain, but they don't want their kids to touch any kind of dirt or anything. I think you get away from reality when you have everything so fine that you want to work in your flower garden without getting your hands muddy. I believe in people keeping clean, but I can't understand why they wouldn't maybe walk around outside with their shoes off. I think people have so many things sometimes, like the kids that are trying to experience dope just to get high. I can get high just looking at a beautiful lake or watching a sunset or looking at the trees blowing in the wind. If they would stop to look at those things, maybe they wouldn't need marijuana to get high on.

For my own children, I want them to have a good education, and I want them to enjoy their lives. I don't want them to get so wrapped up in their work that they can't enjoy all the beauties in nature that I have enjoyed and that we have experienced together. I'd like them not to get all caught up in material things and not to get too keyed up over clothes. Life is too beautiful, and God is too good. He doesn't want us to miss any of it.

Death is going to God. I think fear of death is mostly a fear of the unknown. If you love God and if you live a good life, death to me is more like an experience. Maybe I'm wrong, but I think death is just as natural to us as birth. When we're going, we're afraid, but I think it's like a phase of life. We go from one phase to the other. I mean, it's like a stage. Before you're born, you live in that little world, and then you're born into this world. Then when you leave the earth, you go into another state. It's something like birth. Of course, it could be something altogether different for someone who wasn't a Christian. If they didn't know where they were going, if they didn't love God and all that, it could be a very frightening thing. I was afraid of death for a long time.

LINDA MARTIN

Hamlin, West Virginia.
Occupation: Social worker; campaigner against strip mining.

Divorced and remarried; two children from her first marriage and one from her second.

My dad is a carpenter, and my mother grew up on a farm during the depression. They remember it; it is real to them, whereas it isn't to me. My mother raised me to marry a rich man. It was a subtle preparation: learning how to set the table, how to have polite social talk. She wanted better for me than she had, you know. I went away to college, whereas my mother and father had only gone through the eighth grade. My mother was a smart woman, but she was raised by parents who felt that the woman's place was to get married at fifteen and start having a family. That was what they expected of her, so they wouldn't let her go to high school, even though she was the smartest person in her class. So she wanted that for me. And I wanted it.

I went away to school to meet the ideal fellow. He was in law school, and our relationship was based on wanting the same kind of life. Then it all came quickly: the thirteen-room house with a wine cellar, the country club. I found myself at twenty-nine sitting beside the pool with a lot of other women who were like myself, though they were about forty and their kids were older than mine. Seeing them was like seeing who I would be in a few years.

I had everything that everybody had told would make me happy, right? But it was just so unfulfilling I was miserable. It was a dream; a guy was going to ride up on a white horse. I realized it one day, and said to myself right out, "This is entirely up to me. I have to take over my life right now." It's as if I had moved from my father's house to another man's house, fulfilling everybody else's role expectations. My husband was like my dad. He was generous, but he made the decisions about when we got a car, when we bought a house. I made suggestions, but the decisions were made by him. He controlled the purse strings. What he gave me was more than I needed, but it was a form of control. When I started feeling these things and we discussed them, he would say he couldn't understand me anymore. He was like a child, and he didn't like me changing. He was interested in continuing that lifestyle, and I wasn't. More and more I was aware of sitting in a country club all day when somebody out there was being oppressed by my lifestyle.

I had grown up in West Virginia, and all of a sudden I became very aware I was in another class. I'd been sitting around the dinner table with people who were saying, "What is it those people want?" and I realized they were talking about me. Or we'd be at a cocktail party where everyone was saying, "Nixon is the man," and I'm thinking McGovern.

At any rate, the divorce came, and after a real tough year or so I went back to school in social work. I thought I must be a socialist, because that's how I felt. At first it was just a word, but I was always aware of social justice issues. I was even in the League of Women Voters. I wanted to do something, but I wasn't sure what it was I wanted to do. I just knew it had to be better.

Even during my marriage, I was always against strip mining. He was a banker, a trust officer with clients who were strippers. I went to a strip mining site because I just had to, and he told me I was crazy to go. When I went I ended up with my picture in the paper without a name, and he would get two or three calls about it.

We had lived in Charleston, West Virginia, our whole marriage. After the divorce I went through a period of living alone with the kids, which was really good for me. I was in charge. A lot of women were a big help. I started talking to other women, and I got into a consciousness-raising group. The first night was really tense, and it really got good. It got very heavy, and we were sometimes all in tears on the floor. They were beautiful. The women's consciousness group came the summer I was sitting at the pool saying, "Hey, I've got to do something." By the time I started going through the divorce, they were really a support group. Lots of times I would call them and say, "Hey, I just really need to have some company. Can you come over?" I had a homosexual relationship then, but we both knew we wanted penetration. We're still good friends. I also had an abortion. That was bad; it was like stripmining.

My first husband wouldn't let me nurse my babies. He said it was repulsive. Now that I've given birth to Luke with Julian, it's different. The first time I breast-fed was in the spring. It's like prayer. Everything was budding, and I was able to get Luke outside. It's that same feeling that happens when there is a connection. I feel I am still searching for who I am in a lot of ways. For me, spirituality changes just about every day. It's feeling complete. Sometimes it's a smile between me and Kitty when we understand what each of us is saying to the other without words. She is my best friend because she is still one of those people who often remembers she knows how to fly.

We are going to fight what is going on right here, the stripminers who want to come in and tear up the land here. After they do that, it won't produce anything so that we can feed ourselves. A lot of people living in Lincoln County right now want to grow their own food. We want to live a gentle life on the land and raise a family. If they take our land, we will have to leave, and it is our home. It scares me to death, because already the county where my mom was raised and the one where I grew up are both gone. There is nothing left of them. Lincoln County is the only one in this area of the state where people can still live and farm. The Department of Natural Resources says they don't want to know how we feel about stripmining. Well, I don't have to be an expert to tell them human to human what I've seen stripmining do. It's like those hearings up in Charleston where Rob and I testified. You know, you can't talk to them. Somewhere there is a spark that comes up occasionally where I feel like I can't quit. The day those bulldozers come, I plan to be there, and if there are two hundred people, maybe they won't run us over.

My vision is to change the economic system with communism, not as it exists today, but a system where we will use the land and everything for human needs and not for destruction; where everybody can eat, not just the people who can afford to feed cattle. And where everybody has the freedom to be creative and the time to sit under an apple tree.

GRANDMA STOLTZ

Vashon Island, Washington.
Age: 84.
Education: "Hard Knocks College."

Widowed; mother of two sons, one of whom survives.

You've been through college? I have too. I bet you can't guess the name of my college. Hard Knocks College, and I'm still in it. They won't let me graduate. I'm going to be eighty-four in just a short time, and they won't let me out of it. I got very little education, but I had a lot of schooling at home. My mother had sixteen babies, and she never saw a doctor or a hospital—all midwives. I was the third to youngest. My mother learned that Vaschon Island didn't have a saloon, and that interested her. She came here to visit her family, who had all moved here and were homesteading. She took my youngest brother and me back to Illinois and said to my dad she wanted to move to Vaschon, so he obliged her. They had an auction sale and moved out here. My dad liked a little toddy and would "pal"—you know. That was bad.

I wanted to get an education so badly. I think that was the only time that my mother and I ever had a misunderstanding, when she said I couldn't go to school anymore. I got up in the morning and got my brother's and my lunch, and she said, "You can't go. You are smart enough now." And I said, "I've got to go to school. I just have to get an education." She didn't know any better because she couldn't read or write.

So what education I got I gave myself up there in the attic in that house just north of the Catholic church. We were Lutheran. When I couldn't go to school anymore, I bought this book and went up to that attic every time I had. I wanted to get an education so much, I would have done anything. I worked in people's homes. I loved to go into a strange home and work and see how everybody did things. It was more education for me to see how someone else did everything, and that's the way I learned. When I was about sixteen I went down to work for this family on a big chicken ranch. Well, I was always ambitious, and when I finished my work for the day I'd case up all their eggs for them, which was thirty dozen a case—big wooden cases—and then I'd go to the barn and slide down the shoot. Oh, I was full of the devil. I'd do the same thing today if my legs and my back would hold me up. Well, I'm in love with my legs and back anyway. I don't care what they do. I get around.

We couldn't buy bread or anything on the island in those days. If we wanted to eat, we had to cook it and bake it. I wanted to learn how to bake bread, but my mother said I was too little. I was around twelve and I cooked for my dad, my brothers, and some hired men. When my sister's two children got scarlet fever, my mother made arrangements for some women to come over and bake bread. "The opportunity is here now," I thought. "If I don't take it, it will be gone." I went and got the dry yeast out, and hundred-pound sacks of flour. My mother baked fifteen loaves at a time, and I baked bread and didn't tell anybody. After everybody said how delicious it was, I called the woman and told her not to come back. That's how I was. Very self-sufficient.

I got married when I was twenty because I had too much sympathy. I'd always planned on meeting a girl and traveling with her. Oh, girls, I'd give anything to go with you! I always wanted to follow the croppers, harvesting around the country. We'd have traveled by bus then. Well, he said he'd like to travel too. Baloney! After we were married, he didn't want to travel at all.

I had two sons. One was lost fishing alone off the coast in Alaska. I tell you, I just didn't want to live any longer. But when people are gone, they're gone, and there is nothing more you can do for them. You've got to go on living, so you must not ever let anything like death change your life. Your life was given to you to live. Abide by it, regardless of who dies. My hubby's been gone for six years now, and I live right along.

This trailer is where I sleep and eat, and I have all my sport out in the garden. I don't want anyone to ruin that. I don't care what anyone else does; it's what I do that interests me. Once a fellow wanted to spend the night here with me, and I said, "Don't you talk to me like that. This is my home." I don't care what anyone else would do, but that was too much friendship for me. In my day it was different. Maybe if I'd been smarter and lived that way, I'd have been better off. But I don't like to find fault with anybody. Their life is for them, and I'm living mine.

Yes, I'm still in the College of Hard Knocks. We don't live on a bed of roses, and you take life as it comes. You meet your obstacles, and there are plenty of them. Believe me, there are plenty

of them. Marriage isn't all sunshine. This we confess if we are going
to be honest, though I can't kick too much because I've always
been happy to do what I could. I never live in the past. I didn't ride
a horse, I can't ride a bicycle, and I can't drive a car even if I did
have one. So I'll have to be satisfied with what I've got here, and I
am satisfied.

I don't pay attention to time. Time doesn't mean a thing to me.
I'm not afraid of death, and I'm not thinking this is the last year I'm
going to be growing berries. When I do leave here, I just want to be
cremated. I don't want to have anything to do with a funeral. Once I
went with my mother to buy a casket for one of my brothers who
died. The undertaker sold her a casket she couldn't afford, saying
the neighbors would be impressed to see her son in that fancy
casket. I tell you, you couldn't give me one. I don't want it. I made
up this poem for myself:

When I leave here,
I don't want a flower or a tear.
What I want to hear
Is a cheer
For everyone that's left.

The minister comes here and tries to get me to go to church. I've
got nothing against church, but where could I be closer to God than
right here in my own garden? I can't get any closer. I go out into my
garden at six o'clock in the morning and work until I get hungry. I
don't take a watch with me. When my stomach says eat, I eat.
When I feel like taking a nap, I take one. Sometimes I work out in
my garden the entire day. I don't even stop to look up, because it
hurts my back. My garden is my playfield. I'll grow anything.

I don't know if I was so smart to settle down and get married at
the age of twenty. I denied myself the things I wanted to do. I
wanted to get an education and I wanted to travel, and I haven't
done either one. My hubby would get mad at me if I wouldn't sit in
the house and watch television with him. I'd tell him, "Television
bores me, dad!" My husband was backward about things. He didn't
want responsibility; he didn't even know what it was. I had to do
what I wanted to do because he couldn't see that I was right. He
always said no and believed it couldn't work. I had to deal with the
agricultural department in Washington, D.C., when they told me it
was against the law to have black currants because they cause
white pine blisters. Well, I told them they should come out here and
show me where the white pine is. I'm not afraid of anything just, and

I don't believe in anything unjust. My hubby was always saying not to bother. Well, I did.

We were married fifty years, honey, and I may live yet another fifty myself. I'll live as long as I can and be as happy as a bug in a rug. I just love life. I don't care how it is, I just love it.

I've learned to endure everything, and everything was fun. But when my hubby'd come home with too much, it wasn't fun. As long as he got himself to bed and out of my way, it was all right with me. When you get old enough and get enough brains to develop your thinking and understanding, you're not going to run around after a man because he's not fulfilling his duty.

I think sex is wonderful; it's great. But after so many years, it isn't a necessity. It was just a part of our life. You know. You've had your fling, your endurance, and you're satisfied, and when that came to an end it never bothered me. That's the way it is. He was six years older than me. When you know sex is disappearing, you just kiss it goodbye. It goes when your health goes, I guess. Life comes and goes. That's my idea. When it goes, it's gone.

I just know that I'm so full of life. My legs and my back hurting don't have a thing to do with my life. I would try anything if it would help me to walk. The hardest part of my life was when I lost my son. I couldn't bear it. I didn't think I was going to be able to live. That prayer on the wall is what helped me through. It was delicious, if there is such a thing to say about words. I knew it by heart.

When I was riding on the top of the convertible that Fourth of July, Grandma Morgan and myself, they stopped and asked, "Well, grandmas, what do you want to do now?" I said, "If anybody is going swimming, I want to go too." I never did swim in my life; I'm afraid of the water. But that was the first thing that came to my mind. We were having a fair for the Fourth of July.

It's just wonderful to have such friends. I count my blessings on both hands and feet, and I don't have enough fingers or toes to count them all. I have so much to be thankful for. Oh, I'm telling you, people are so wonderful, and you are meeting people of every type. I'd give anything to go with you girls. If I had the ability to walk, I'd just pick up and go and wouldn't wait for anybody.

CHAPTER FOUR:
DOING JUSTICE

"Our mother house here in the Potomac area is one of my big energy investments now. The question is, what is the future of the building, a fortress like this? It's also the question of holding some very expensive land in one of the richest areas in the country, and the symbolism of that. So that is another opportunity to make some real, substantive moves that will greatly influence our future. Theresa Cain is our general administrator, and after moving out of the hinterlands, she sees that the future is being much more in an urban office rather than a suburban or country office like this.

——Betty Barrett, Maryland

MARY LUKE TOBIN

"As we become more aware of the kind of world that exists now and its enormous inequities, we are forced into the question, "Who is God in a world of evil?" When I faced that question, I came to look at what I really believed, and that's why I feel that if I'm going to really say I'm Christian, then I have to know how and why that fits into what I see. There are women and fellow theologians who are not Christian. Basically, it's a belief in a transcendent God who calls us to justice, and I believe that the exemplar is Jesus Christ and that hearing the cry of the oppressed is the cry of the gospels. That is what God is."

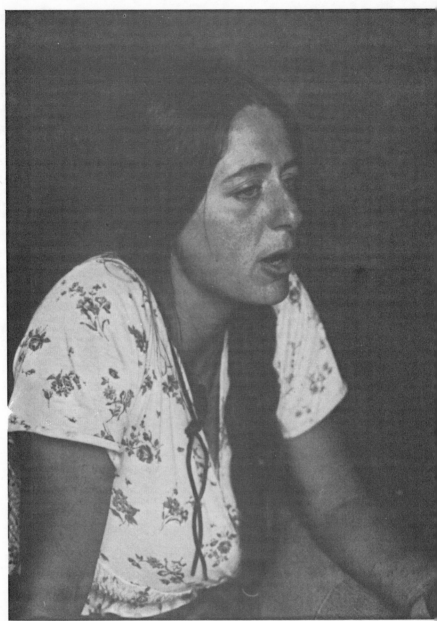

DONNA BOUCHARD "Women seem to be stronger than men. They have had to struggle so long and hard to be considered equal that there is a strength there that most men don't have."

"I think everybody has a personal death or revolution."
(Betty Barrett)

BETTY BARRETT

Potomac, Maryland.
Occupation: Administrator, Mercy
Sisters; former president, St. Xavier's
College, Chicago, Illinois

Age: 57.

Institutions are the things that need to change. I'm still searching for an answer to the question that exists in my own being: Is the only way you can solve everything really by living with the poor and serving the poor directly—and as a consequence giving up your institutions? Or, is there a possibility of getting the voice of the poor into the institutions? Institutions are politics. When you are in the institution, it is very difficult to really see how in many cases you are oppressing the poor.

We Mercy Sisters are talking about a shared services corporation, so that some services can more effectively be provided by a network of institutions. In a sense, it's a power position. For example, if you are going to change the whole approach to health care in hospitals, the only way is to have a strong enough institutional base, a large enough group of people who say, "We want to do it this way." If you network, you can do things, and if you don't, you let bureaucracy creep in. The poor are the only ones that can bring the message. That is the one thing I want to test: is it possible that we can really trust and believe each other in developing a two-way communication between the grassroots and the power structure? I think we've begun to squash the pyramid of the institutions that we run and make them more like a circle.

My whole experience has been within the establishment, and I believe in the institutions, but not as they exist now. The institution does something to you. I had the experience of being at the bottom of the seniority totem pole in the college system I was in. Then all of a sudden I became the president of that college. I thought everybody was treating me the same way, but I didn't realize that I was only getting half the message. I thought I was still the same person as when I was the radical junior member of the faculty, but there is something that the structure does to people. We are not the same person once we step into a power position.

I'm interested in the institutions for structural changes. I keep being convinced philosophically that you can spend the rest of your life trying to change people's attitudes, but if you change only a few systems, people will have to behave differently, and their attitudes will change. I am convinced that that is the way to do it. I say don't change everybody's attitudes so that then they will change the system, just change the systems. Washington provides that opportunity, so it is worth the effort of being here. It is the opportunity to make some moves and have some influence on decisions that will greatly affect our future.

In the Eighth Day Center's legislative action, I was one of the organizers of Bread for the World in Chicago, and I've maintained that relationship here. When I arrived last year, I was just in time for the farm bill that was going through the House of Representatives. Bread for the World had spent a lot of time on the grain reserves, so I got in for one week of active lobbying and was there when the bill finally passed. It's nice to win, you know. I have been able to develop quite a relationship with a congressperson from this district and the two senators. Being right here, you don't have to just write letters. You can go knock on the door and say, "Remember me?" Monday I will visit them because of the ERA. The big ERA rally is Sunday, you know. I haven't had the time to be the instigator, so I've been the responder. At the Eighth Day Center I could plan strategy and try to move people, and I miss that. Of course, most of the time you ended up doing it yourself.

Truth is everybody's responsibility. Today, a religious college must see itself as an institution seeking and finding the truth. In many cases, especially in social justice issues, this truth will bring confrontation with some of the positions of the church. It is the college's responsibility to affirm the church and at the same time to confront the church when it is found to be in contrast with the truth.

Religious communities have the same responsibility of pushing forward the truth. The way you push it forward is to seek it, and if necessary to confront it, even to the point of dissent. For example, the whole area of medical ethics, the issue of sterilization. This is a real problem for many hospitals because of the very rigid stand of the church on sterilization. Women's ordination is another issue. All of my relationships have been caught up totally in the church world, though I don't think religious communities have to be. They should also be caught up with the "real" world. That could make for a really powerful body.

Most religious women are sensitive to the ERA and are very supportive of it. The terrible thing in the church is what has happened between lay and religious women. I don't know if we became too professional or if we ran too far ahead. Most of the laywomen were educated by religious women, and many of those gals are not even the least bit sensitive to ERA. There seems to be a real separation between religious women and Catholic laywomen. Something happened that moved us apart. Elizabeth McAllister (the woman who married Phil Berrigan) said once, "They ran so far ahead in the peace movement that people didn't have a chance to catch up with them. And they didn't make any efforts to pull the others along. How far can you go without leaving too many behind?"

We religious women are a strange group. We are so highly prepared to be professionals, and we are achievers. Yet we have so moved into the establishment that it is difficult to become poor with the poor. I think the tax exemption is one thing that made it possible for us to be so much a part of the establishment, and maybe it was not a good thing. For example, this place: we could never have held this land here in Potomac for all these years without tax exemptions. It is very difficult for us to be a pilgrim people. Our professionalism gets in the way, and so does our property, our holdings. That's the question. Do you hold on to these institutions, or do you get out of them? I say try to change the institutions so that they respond. There will always be institutions, so what would we achieve by giving them up?

I think everybody has a personal death or revolution. Mine came while I was president of St. Xavier's, a small college in Chicago, in the late sixties. I had come from a world that was very solid. Everything was in its place, even in my childhood neighborhood, where no one ever moved away—very structured. And I was caught in it. Then the sixties came, and one Christmas I sent out a card that expressed my feelings. The words on the front were "Silent Night, Holy Night," mixed with blacks (Selma and so on) and the inside had the word "Peace," but it was broken right in half. And that was exactly how I felt, because my world at that point felt broken.

After Vatican II, the church seemed to undergo excruciating pain. Religious communities were being disrupted, and so was the college campus. Every day I had an explosion. The civic society

was all caught up in the black-white situation. We lived in a
neighborhood where the college was surrounded by great
prejudice. The agony of finding out that the good guys — the civic
government, the church — were not so good led to a realization that
society could not go on the way it was, and wasn't supposed to. I
think Teilhard de Chardin was a big influence; he was read with
great interest then. I began to look around me, and I saw a
continuation of his ideas. It was out of all that that I knew I couldn't
go on doing nothing. My mother said, "You've given up being
president of the college to do something, but what have you
succeeded in doing?" I said, "Not much, but I know I should be
trying." I think I still have that feeling. I'm not sure why I'm here, but
I know I should be trying to make the world change. It's not
supposed to be this way.

The world I grew up in was full of "right" places and
"right"answers. What I stepped into at St. Xavier's College was a
world in which the kids knew if they demonstrated they would
change the rules and regulations. They were changing structures.
These kids changed me. When I was little, the adult world of my
parents, aunts, and uncles had things in it that I didn't like, but I
didn't expect to change anything, just not to be a part of it. Well,
after being with those college kids, I saw things could change. I
don't think I'll live to see it. In fact, sometimes I cry because I'm as
old as I am, and I don't think I'm going to see a lot of this, but I feel
it is going to happen in time: the kingdom, the transformation of
society. There must be a little Jew in me: the kingdom is here, right
now. So you keep plowing through a few miserable things.

I had a front-page battle with Archbishop Cody during his first
year. We were going to have a theological symposium at St.
Xavier's. We had succeeded in getting Karl Rahner, Johann Metz,
Edward Schillebeeck, Yves Congar, Charles Davis, and Jean
Danilou to come to this little tiny college campus and sit down to
talk to people for four days. Cody told me that I couldn't have it: it
was not in keeping with the norms for ecumenical activities for the
archdiocese. So I had to write to the faculty and explain that the
archbishop didn't want us to have this forum. We were going to
have some other institution take on the symposium. It was breaking
my heart. Well, one of the faculty members took the letters to the
National Catholic Reporter. Commonweal got it, and
so did the front pages of the *Daily News* and the *Tribune.*
"ARCHBISHOP DENIES COLLEGE THE RIGHT TO

HAVE SYMPOSIUM." He denied that he had denied us the right. After four or five days of telephone calls with everyone saying, "We're right there behind you," I started saying, "I'd rather somebody would be right up here with me, or even in front of me." Cody said it was a misunderstanding. So the faculty said, "Let's have it rather than lose our integrity as a college community." So we had it. We expected three or four hundred people, and we had fifteen hundred. We had to have closed-circuit TV and everything else.

I never stood in the good graces of the cardinal the rest of my time at the college. In fact, a reporter friend of mine would occasionally say, "Why is it that the other four Catholic college presidents were invited by the archbishop to such and such and you were not?" Sister Ann Ida, the president of Mundelein, wasn't invited either. She is the only college president who during the turmoil allowed her statement to be quoted with her name. It was, of course, a bold, supportive statement.

It was hard. I don't think I had a faith crisis, though. It gave me a depth of soul that I would never have had otherwise. Cody wasn't the church to me. I think the priests and religious and lay folks in Chicago have wasted an awful lot of energy in the last ten years spinning wheels. They should go ahead and do, instead of sitting and waiting. I never pulled out because I get my greatest support in what I call now community life. What we had before was only common life, but what I see religious life growing into is what keeps me going. I can't really be me without some sort of self-fulfillment, and yet I can't really be me without also giving myself away. It's a strange thing—a being and giving balance. It's impossible to be a human being without giving yourself away to some extent. I was greatly loved as a child, and maybe that is why I emphasize in my own life the other aspect. I have learned that every human being is scratched, and some people are so scratched you wonder how they can even hold up their heads. I like to give, so religious life has been easy for me.

After I left the college, I worked for the government for five years. That was during the days of civil rights, and those were kind of my Camelot days. I worked with the education department in the Chicago office. I never thought of this before, but the religious community wasn't important to me then. I found another community while I was licking my wounds, the Education Department of the Human Relations community. The director was a beautiful woman, a fantastic, mod WASP. She and I continued to

be friends through the years. Also on the commission were a
beautiful black man, an orthodox Jew, and myself in my short blue
habit. When we went to southern Illinois, we represented
everything they hated.

I had walked out on the college, and they were obvious about
not supporting me. When it came time to make the move, I knew it
was right. I didn't even stop to think about the fact that I was
probably one of the first religious women in our province to resign
from a canonical appointment. (I was appointed president by a fiat
from the provincial. I was called over to the provincial house one
day and asked if I was still interested in the Better World
Movement. I had volunteered to go to South America, and I
thought this was my chance, but they said they were going to send
the president of Xavier off to be the American director of the
Better World Movement, and that I was going to take her place.
And that was how I was going to help Better World.) When I
resigned, no one had ever done that before.

I have felt total abandonment, but there has always been a place
to move. When that stops, there will really be abandonment. After I
finished working for the state, I created the job of commissioner for
human relations for myself. I had been a commissioner while I was
president of the college—a governor's appointment—so I knew
what they were doing. I wanted to do it too, so I talked to the
director of the commission and created the job. I imagine real
abandonment will come. I'm sure it will, because that is what the
full development is. I hope the development comes with being able
to let go.

I always feel like I am running out of time. Probably my greatest
concern—and people are always kidding me about this—is the fact
that I cannot accept my age. When I see young women who are
just beginning, I want so to be there, and that's a terrible thing.
Each day, it's hard to imagine that this body is really mine and that
it's aging. I'm fifty-seven. It's as though things are moving so fast,
and you are not going to be there when it's finished. I still never
think much of my own death. I just cry because I'm growing older. I
want to go on and on and on. I suppose all this tremendous activity
I'm involved in is a sort of running from something, probably from
that inside, deep-down thing that I don't want to look at underneath.
I've been described as a workaholic, but not as an efficient one. I'm
a great spinner of wheels.

When I was living in Chicago, I knew a lot of people and had a lot of connections. Moving here, I had to rebuild all that. There are great cultural things here in Washington, and when I first came here I had time for the first time in years. But I didn't know many people, so they weren't calling me up to go places.

I am not sure what the future of religious life holds. I am sure that it will be a much smaller group of women, and I have great hopes that it will be a group who work at bringing justice. I think we have misused our freedom, our poverty, our celibacy, and our obedience. It should have been a freeing thing, so that we could do the work of the kingdom, but we haven't. We've structured ourselves into almost idiotic things. We have the opportunity for such freedom, but we are all so wounded. I don't know if the bodies can be moved along as a whole.

The Sisters of Notre Dame in Boston have split in two groups, and in Baltimore there is a group that is ready to split. What happens is that the group that is more actively inclined, that talks about ministry of influence rather than ministry of service, dissipates, disappears, and leaves behind the other. I see no real benefit in canonical status; that isn't an essential in religious life. However, I don't know what kind of longevity those who have moved away have. Canonical status is obeying canon law, the way Rome says, but even the rewritten canon law is not very good. The five principles stated at the beginning are beautiful, but then the very canons that follow deny the principles just enunciated. So, if canon law gets in the way too much, I have no problem with . . . !

I am running out of time, you know. I can't wait forever. That is where my hope gets frayed around the edges: when I see the great spectrum of people in our religious communities and wonder whether we can move them sufficiently to bring new life. Or do we hold on to the old so long that we die? They talk about charity at home and caring for the elderly, but that's not what we came for. We came for the other thing. We are a very old community, but my natural inclination is to run ahead. I keep dreaming about being a part of a grand plan.

What you consistently need when you are in a power position, and I don't have, is constant feedback. I am convinced that we are so addicted to structures that we begin to perform like structures. It's like a self-fulfilling phophecy. We have made some horrible mistakes affecting people with our collegial model while we have been crushing the pyramid into a circle. That is why I want to get to the voices of the poor. Lots of times we talk about oppressive structures, but what we need is a voice to tell us, "This is when it is good, and this is when it is bad."

This is a microcosm of society. We talk about structural change as a form of justice. I think the sisters of the United States have done the most successful job of structural change in religious life that has ever been done. It was a very unjust system. We took the principle of the dignity of the individual human being, and we looked at the system and said, "It doesn't comply. It really is not just." So we change it. To the folks that don't like the change in the system, I say, "We made one big change only. We looked at what was the dignity of each of us, and we saw that the system adhered to that."

What we haven't done is taken the principle of relationship between the unique me and the unique you and dealt with it as well. Because that puts limits on my freedom. If we take that first tenet of the Declaration of Independence, it really is that I am unique and so are you, and I've got to respect you and you've got to respect me. If we do that, we have freedom, liberty, and so on. The relation of it is that giving yourself away aspect.

Sixteen years from now, come back and I'll have all the answers. I live in hope because of today. I met two beautiful young women who give me a lot of hope. When you look back at the movies of the twenties, thirties, and forties and then you look at the movies today, you see a mode of reflection in today's movies that you don't see in the others. I think much of my life has been spent without reflecting deeply on experience. I tend to be more of an intuitive/idea person. I don't examine back; it always tends to be forward for me. I haven't reflected on the deep down inside of me that much; isn't that strange? And I've had a very rich life . . . I could have had a lot of good reflections. It's been hard. It's been beautiful. It's been good.

MARY LUKE TOBIN *Denver, Colorado*
Occupation: Former president,
Leadership Conference of Women
Religious. The only American woman
invited to Vatican II.

Age: 70.

I'm on my way up to Ring Lake Ranch, which is a summer
extension of the University of Denver Divinity School. I'm teaching
a course on women in the church, a subject in which I'm very
interested. In the fall, I'll be teaching one on Thomas Merton. He
was a personal friend of mine, and I've been giving lots of courses
on him, since this is the tenth anniversary of his death. I'm starting a
Thomas Merton center here in Denver next year. What I hope to
do is to take Thomas's quotes on nuclear disarmament and print
them in a leaflet, then have dozens of professionals from various
disciplines discuss them and thereby be involved in a process of
synergism. Thomas Merton was excited that people could get new
insights from each other, and he felt that the contemplative had to
get this kind of contact. He was going to set up a center, but he
died, so after ten years, I'm going to do it. Basically, he had about
ten themes, and I'm going to take the primary ones. Nuclear
destruction and the oppression of women are good places to begin.
We have to start with widening and discovering alternatives. We
can't simply stand around and not try to find alternative ways of
doing something about the enormous inequities in the world. We
have to look at the marginal women, the women on the fringes. Our
women are thirsting for spirituality.

Someone said to me once, "How can you be in favor of a man
who wrote in sexist language?" I said, "Read my writing ten years
ago. It was totally sexist." We were all into that. We didn't even
know it—incredible, but we didn't. But Merton was open and saw
through many injustices. Once he got together a group of
contemplative prioresses because he saw their situation as being so
oppressed. They were not even allowed to get together for
meetings. He began urging them to do and be what they had to be

and not live their lives with such enormous oppression hanging over their heads. They had to take their courage in their hands and go, and they went. There they were, just knowing what they had to do.

I have some friends who are contemplatives who are very deeply concerned with the problems of the world. Now, that's the only kind of contemplative that I can see: one who, through means of a life of very serious, sincere, profound reflection, can see herself in terms of carrying the concerns of the world in her heart. I think there is a very special attraction to that kind of life, and there are some people who deeply feel it. The person who has a strong attraction to a way of life that searches for truth and praises God is doing something. And I think human life of doing things simply, is a way of being far more aware than most. That is important: that constant awareness that we all should have. I know people who live that type of life with great purity of heart and great profundity and commitment, and I thoroughly respect it. Merton was a great contemplative, but he seemed so ordinary. He enjoyed talking about the problems of the world, although he felt his own search must include solitude. Looking at his gifts and talents and what his life was, he felt he came together best with his life of solitude and his writing and developing the intellectual life.

There are circumstances and conditions of our lives that help us to make decisions on the expending of our energy and where we find ourselves. We don't come at these things from a pure vacuum: we're somewhere and we're with some people and we need certain people. True, you can just do so much, but I think one of the factors in prioritizing is your own history, your own talents, and what you see you've got to bring to this world that we're involved in: the creation of a more human world.

When I went to Vatican II, I was convinced that women should participate in the decisions that affect their lives, and from that time until this I've been working in one way or another on that particular issue, as well as all the issues of participation, justice, and oppression. I think that is what we have to be up to. People don't even get to decision-making if they are totally oppressed. They don't get to the level of survival, or even a human situation. So many people are suffering from not having that. All the justice issues are involved in whatever the church is up to, and the "women's issue" is just one of them. I call myself a Christian feminist because I think

the themes of Christianity as they are revealed in the New
Testament gospels have to do with all kinds of liberation. That's why
women belong to the group of the oppressed: they are unliberated.
It's hard to tell people that, because they don't see American
women as oppressed. I think it's true, judging by our economic
standards as a people, that we don't have the kind of oppression
that exists in the Third World countries, where women are really at
the bottom of the totem pole. But nevertheless, women are second-
class citizens here.

I was the only American woman invited to Vatican II. I was invited
because I was the head of the Leadership Conference of Women
Religious. Cardinal Suenans stood up in the council and said, "Why
is it we are addressing only half the church?" They said, "Sure we
are," and then invited these fifteen women.

It was a very exciting time, if you can imagine what it was like:
fifteen sisters and twenty-five hundred men, who were bishops and
theologians. They didn't know what to do with us or what to make
of us. I was fully habited, as was every other nun in the world at
that time. We were all invited as "auditors," and we were not to
speak. Bernard Harring pushed until he got three of us appointed to
commissions, and we then had a chance to speak, not on the floor,
but within the commission that prepared the document for the
bishops to vote on. The few times I spoke it was mainly on the participation of women in those decisions that have to do with our
lives. That was brewing way back then. I was so naive I thought
they would be delighted that we women wanted to participate in
decisions that affected our lives. Well, they were not delighted at all.
Not at all. And so the struggle started, and we are still in it, of
course.

But that really started things for American religious women; we
began to move rapidly after that. These women have done a
fantastic job of taking hold of their own lives, and I think they have
done it through some hard struggles — all of this is in the past ten
years. Prior to that it was unheard of for religious women to wear
ordinary clothes, or to live and travel as they pleased. But they
decided it was theirs to do, so they took hold and did it. That is a
fantastic story, I think. Just that one factor: taking hold of the
decisions that control their own lives.

There are still all these other things yet to do, but we have an
opportunity. Just from the nature of our lives, we are given a lot of
leeway in society. People like nuns. Nuns can get jobs because

people are delighted to have them. This is part of the payoff of what
our lives have been, part of the dedication, if you will, and the
intensity and thoroughness with which we have taken things on. It
has paid off. We have made the most of opportunities we have had,
and with the kind of freedom we've had I think we've really done
some remarkable things. We have learned we can do it.

There can't be barriers between laywomen and religious women,
but there still are. I am just delighted about our work with
laywomen. I think we must be inclusive rather than exclusive.

The young sisters from many communities say to me, "Our older
sisters are magnificent, but it is the ones who are in their forties and
fifties that don't understand." It's not hard for the old people to
understand; they were pioneers in their day. So we just proceed.
We start with the men. The pain will do them good. We went
through it, and it did us all good. We go through pain when we
change. When it gets inside, then you have to do something about
it. It is costly, but we cannot be held back by dead wood. I don't
believe in being brutal or harsh, but I think we should do all we can
to raise consciousness. We all have seen fruits from our own
oppressors.

I am on the task force for women's ordination. We are getting
ready for a meeting in November. It has to happen. We just have to
keep the struggle going and not expect that someone up there or
out there is going to do it for us. Women have to be ordained
because of the injustice of the situation now, but I don't know how
long it will take. The church as a community of the faithful has got
to have much fuller participation on the part of all the people, and a
far fuller listening to and hearing them in decision-making. All of that
is impossible now. I think it all has to happen, but it is going to take
a long time. In the meantime, I don't think women should be
excluded. There are some women who are willing to go into that
system. Maybe they will change it.

As we become more aware of the kind of world that exists now
and its enormous inequities, we are forced into the question, "Who
is God in a world of evil?" When I faced that question, I came to
look at what I really believed, and that's why I feel that if I'm going
to really say I'm Christian, then I have to know how and why that
fits into what I see. There are women and fellow theologians who
are not Christian. Basically, it's a belief in a transcendent God who
calls us to justice, and I believe that the exemplar is Jesus Christ

and that hearing the cry of the oppressed is the cry of the gospels. That is what God is.

I have to work that out, just as each of us does, and I find that the great invitation (that we have not heeded) is to restore the inequities of the world. That is what I think our faith ought to be concerned with, and we ought to get about it. You know, sitting on the tracks is one way. I've been out to Rocky Flats. I got very much into the antiwar movement. I was in Vietnam twice and in jail a couple of times, so all of that same kind of thing flows together out of spirituality. I met a lot of wonderful people there, too. It's good support to find other people in there that see it as you see it. That is the kind of thing that is a sign of hope, that others are doing this; and that's where you want to be found, in that kind of company. Maybe that's all we can do—just put our little two cents in here and there and wherever our efforts take us—because, well . . . I think the first Christians had to throw it in too.

DONNA BOUCHARD *Rocky Flats, Colorado.*
Occupation: Antinuclear activist;
member of the Truth Force; secretary.
Education: Secretarial school.

Divorced, mother of one daughter.

I was raised a Catholic for a while. Right now I would say I am
Christian; I believe in the Lord Jesus. We lived for a time in
Lexington and Concord, Massachusetts. I have two younger
brothers and an older sister who has several children. I took a two-
year course in secretarial school. I guess if I can't find any other
work, I can always find secretarial work.

Last year I was working as a secretary and putting much of my
energy into getting my daughter back. I lost custody of her on the
grounds that I was an unfit mother, which was not true, but the
people that were working against me were very political. It wasn't so
much me, but her father and her father's crimes. His father had
designed the nuclear guidance system on missiles, and so he was
really into this nuclear stuff. Because of my father-in-law's social
position and the political influence he had in court, he also got
custody of my child for ten months. He had complete control of the
whole situation, even to preventing any chance of my parents having
temporary custody. So most of my energy was directed to trying to
get her back. That was in Massachusetts. Finally, about two months
ago, they gave her to her father, and she's doing well.

My daughter is four years old now. Her name is Christie, and she
is really beautiful and I love her a lot. I've been doing a lot of thinking
now about whether I should go back, which probably means nine-to-
five, rather useless and menial secretarial work, so I am allowed to
get my child back. Or is it more important to be here at Rocky Flats,
knowing that she is being really well taken care of because she is
back with her father? That is one step in the right direction, and also
he is the one I really trust is taking good care of her.

Right now, I'm into the antinuclear thing, which has something to
do with the problem I had in court when I lost custody. I also want
to work with people in mental institutions and jails, to help get out
those that don't belong there. Some people get sentenced to life,

maybe on a drug charge, and were drugged so heavily they didn't even know they were being put there. There are also people getting out of jail after multiple murders, and at the same time others are being kept in jail for political reasons such as trying to save the world from nuclear attacks. That is crazy. I've got six friends right now that are in jail for protesting here at Rocky Flats and for trying to stop the construction of nuclear bombs.

I started with the Crimshaw Line and went to Seabrook. They were pretty well organized, so I started following the antinuclear movement. I'm committed to it. A lot of people don't understand. The question is not whether we will get radiation poisoning—we *are* getting poisoned! The media have not been letting the public know of all the dangers of nuclear plants, especially those at Rocky Flats. I just started getting involved here this summer, and when I learned of all the implications of this place, I wanted everybody to know about it. People who live here are putting their lives on the line every day. Eleven thousand acres of ground around here are contaminated. The air we breathe is contaminated. Where we are sitting right now is a target: if there were a nuclear attack, we would be one of the first to go. I think it's insanity to produce bombs.

We are doing this because we want to bring attention to this place, and once people become aware of all the dangers, we hope to get more people to ask more questions about it, and to ask why we are doing what we are doing. The hardest thing to do is to spread the word about a place like Rocky Flats. I just feel right now that is where my energies should be directed. I feel like I have a lot of strength in me to make a change.

I am also very interested in the Indians of our country, and I've always felt a spiritual closeness to the Indian culture. I think they really have a good way of life. I am interested in the Indians' point of view about this world, how their world existed before the white man came in to change their whole culture, saying, "Be white men now." They tried to take away the Indians' rituals and what they considered sacred, and then they put them on reservations.

There is such a communication gap between what's happening in the government and the people of this country. The news media only let us know what they want us to know. To me, being lied to is worse than physical violence. The Truth Force has literature on a lot of these things in order to let people know what's going on, so they can be alive to enjoy it. The word has to be spread personally. The truth is coming out more and more, though. People are spending their lives for this country. The Indians in their Longest Walk walked from California to the capitol in Washington. People are protesting nuclear energy at the power plants; the people of Rocky Flats Truth Force are sitting on the tracks to keep the trains from coming in where triggers are made for nuclear bombs.

Sitting here at the tracks is a little different from being back at the house where our headquarters are located. Back there in the group, there is a tendency to slip into stereotyped roles. Right now, we see a need to get more organized as a force, and we started at the meeting last night. We talked about the Truth Force being dominated by men. At meetings and so on, men just take over. There are some strong women that are not here right now, however. Women seem to be stronger than men. They have had to struggle so long and hard to be considered equal that there is a strength there that most men don't have.

It's important because we are in an arrest situation here, and several of us are in jail right now for protesting on the tracks. Every time another train comes through, about twice a week, we face arrest when we sit on the tracks to stop it from going into the nuclear power plant.

I think women can be more compassionate and sensitive, and as a group can reach a higher level of consciousness than men and women together or even men as a group. When we were at Seabrook, we had a feminist speaker at a rally, and she was beautiful. She referred to nuclear power plants as raping the earth.

I've never been raped. I've been humiliated, and at one point I thought it might become rape, but it didn't. That was when I was in high school. I was on a date, and I wanted to go home but he wouldn't take me. He just humiliated me, and sometimes I wonder if that wasn't even worse than being raped. I felt really bad and I hated him. I wished all kinds of awful things would happen to him. Two weeks later, he was in an accident and was paralyzed from the waist down, and then I really felt bad.

ANN FLAGG   *(Tacoma, Washington.) Occupation: Sister of St. Joseph of Peace. Advocate for disadvantaged. Age: 58.*

I live by myself. The girls knew I was there, and they also knew that they could come at any time in the night. I have no intention of trying to change them; I just want them to know there is a place to go. Maybe twice a week a girl would come in, sometimes drunk, and sleep, and then go when it got light. I work in the Martin Luther King Center as an advocate, and that's how I'd get to know them. I'd get sent out to homes, and then they'd come in to see me.

Most of these girls are Indians. They have no place to go. Often a battered wife will come to stay here for a while. Once a man from a mental institution who had nowhere to go stayed with me. Those are the kind of people I want—the ones with no place to go. It always bothered me when the police or hospitals said there was noplace. One time there was a man who came in the freezing winter. He had nothing, and we gave him a blanket and a hat, and he left. Well, that's the kind I want. They don't want anything big, just an overnight deal. I have talked with prostitutes I know, mostly Indians. Not the ones with pimps, but the ones who are prostitutes because they need a place to sleep for a few dollars. They are not professionals.

This is my baby. I love this house. I'll be fifty-nine, and I've waited to do something like this since 1940. I've always been happy with what I did, but this is different: this is the most beautiful, interesting place there is, because you can't say what you do. It's different every day. You don't plan ahead, you just let it happen. It's kind of where I wanted to be all my life, and it's what I believed in when I became a Sister of Peace. These people have to know they have a place, and that's what's driving me.

When I first became a sister, I was taking everybody else's word about what God's will was. Then we got into this discernment thing. I didn't like the idea at all, but I finally got through it, and now you couldn't make me choose anything else. I read a lot and listen to community meetings, though I pretend I don't. I fight like the devil, saying I don't like this change and that change, and finally in the end I like it. I found change very hard. I didn't like the change from the

Latin mass, and I didn't like the change in our community office
prayers. But now, I would never go back. Oh, God, no!

When I first came to the convent, I was a teacher. I was lousy at
it, and I knew I couldn't teach any longer. I wanted to work with the
poor. My provincial told me if I found a place and found a job, she
would back me all the way. I came to this parish and asked for a
classroom, and Father gave me this old house. The retarded and
the poor were all just walking the streets with no place. Sister Joan
was interested in doing this for a long time, so she came with me. I
asked her, and she sent her truck here two weeks later. We solicit
donations to keep this house going. This is the kind of thing I have
been looking for and the reason I wanted to be a nun.

The last two years of teaching were getting hard. I used to go to
the homes at night, poor Mexican people in San Fernando, and I
loved them. They were so poor and so beautiful. But then I was getting older, and I knew teaching was getting harder. The kids were
getting harder to handle, and everything I read was about the poor.
I just knew I had to do it, and my community was beautiful about it.
So God keeps sending things.

As far as the future goes, I don't know. I just hope we are all
Christians, working together for the poor. Religious life? Commitment to church? Marriage? I don't know. I don't understand those
things anyway. I don't see any difference. That's the kind of thing I
don't like to think about. We spend a lot of time thinking when we
could be doing. Five years from now is too far away for me to think
about. When I first came here I thought this was what I was going
to be doing forever, but now I know I'll never be satisfied. I've come
to accept that about myself. At first, I thought that was terrible and
I hated myself for it, but now I realize that's the way I am and that's
it. I know eventually I would like to end up working with the mentally ill, but there are a lot of things I must do first. I do think they
are the most needy people there are.

I wouldn't like to see religious life end. I don't know how it will be;
I leave it to the Lord. There is such a need for it. I think there
always have to be people who don't have other obligations for service. Now I might change my mind about that, but I do see a value to
it. To tell the truth, I am not petrified that it is all going to stop. For
me, I love the community and I wouldn't want it to fall apart. I think
what we are doing is great, and I don't fear the future. I do fear,
however, someone saying to me that I can't do this anymore.

It wasn't until 1969 that we were called by the Pope to have a

chapter. He said to go back to our original spirit. We started looking
at Mother Clare, the foundress. She was in England and saw the
Irish girls coming there and being exploited. She wanted to help
them adjust to the big cities, so she started houses and places
where they could come. She was an Anglican nun and felt dissatis-
fied that they were not considering the poor at all, so she left and
became a Poor Clare. Then she began a lot of writing about political
situations and the oppression of the poor. Anyway, she ended up
leaving the Poor Clares and founding an order of women who would
work with the poor. She went to visit the Pope for approval, and he
encouraged her in every way. It was during the time of the famine in
Ireland, and she did a lot of work there. She started talking to
bishops, and things went from bad to worse. They were not interested at all. She began talking about the church and its lack of
understanding for the needs of the poor, and I guess the bishops
were telling her to go someplace else. People in Ireland knew that
she kept many of them from dying. She finally said, "In no way is
this community of women going to be able to do anything as long as
I am their leader." So she left, very discouraged, and asked another
woman to take her place. Eventually, the community was invited to
Takoma to work.

We have begun looking at Mother Clare's writings and are realizing what she has been saying. They focus mainly on the injustices of
the church, the poor and the powerless, and women—very much on
women. Most of her books were condemned, and so they weren't
published. We have a few old copies.

I can compare her to Mother Teresa, whom I love and would
want to work with, but I think Mother Teresa is a little bit backwards in the church. She believes in organized religious institutions.
You know, we all pray together at the same time and all wear habits
and all that. Maybe where she is, habits are necessary. I think she is
wonderful, but I don't want to go back to habits again or pray at the
same time as everybody else. What difference does it make if your
habit is trailing in the dust or isn't? I think we worry about the
wrong things.

One of the things I thought was neat about Mother Clare was
that she was a woman who would not consider security as an important thing. So she would do what she thought was right even
though it brought about all kinds of difficulties for our community. I
think that is really meaningful, because that is what we should be
looking for now. We are very fearful because we are still saying our

community has got to survive. But it doesn't have to survive. It will
and should survive only if we are doing what is just. And that is
hard to do. We are always worried about finances and about how to
increase our numbers instead of what we can do to bring about
social justices, what we can do to end oppression in the world.
We're getting to that, but we are slow. That's what made her great:
the fact that she wasn't concerned about her own security. If we
could just hear that message for ourselves now. In those days, the
nuns went into the bars. They were really with the people. We got
away from that because of the organization. In the beginning we
were with the poor, supported by a little magazine called *Offmill*. It
was low intellectually, but those were the kind of people we went
out to and those were the people who supported us. Everybody
can't be an intellectual. Those other people, they are what they are.

I just know that anytime anyone comes up with a change I get
afraid, and I don't pay attention for a while. But I really do. I don't
like to condemn people who are afraid, because I know what it feels
like. I was going to be the last one who took off the veil. I was never
going to wear slacks, and now I don't have any skirts! I never tried
to analyze it in any way. I think our community is tremendous in
that we didn't have to have everybody change at the same time.
When I had my silver jubilee, I was sent to get my hair done for the
first time as a surprise from the kids. When I came back I couldn't
put the veil back on because it would have messed up my hair, and
I just never wore the veil again. After that, I didn't have to wear it.
It's what I said, to be people that made the difference. The only
thing that makes me different from other women is that I have the
word "sister" tacked onto my name. And sometimes things are
much easier for me because of it.

MARY JO SHANNON *(Seattle, Washington.) Occupation: Director, Campaign for Human Development; staff member, archdiocesan task force. Residence: parish rectory. Age: 28.*

Single.

I am the second oldest of nine brothers and sisters. One child that has lived with us for the last eight years is deaf. My father is a social worker for the state, and my mother is, well, a very interesting woman. Now she's into an interdenominational pentecostal group, in some sense definitely charismatic. I think it's really different in that they are into women being in the home, but she's happy and I respect it. She was ill for a long time, and she felt that she had been healed. We were a family-centered group. My father worked for twenty years for a tobacco company, and then they let him go. They had promoted him to some kind of position that meant he would travel, and he decided it was more important to be at home, so they said goodbye. It was definitely my mother's priority to have him around. Money has never been an important thing.

I am a diocesan director for the Campaign for Human Development. I do that half time, and the rest of the time I work as a staff person for the archdiocesan task force. Both of the jobs I do out of the Office of Catholic Charities, especially as it relates to justice education. My B.A. is in social work, and from there I worked for three years at Bellarmine High School in Tacoma, running a community service program where students did volunteer work with different agencies. I am about three-fourths done with my master's in administration. My focus will be specifically on justice issues.

There are very few women who work professionally in the diocese. I've gone through some interesting changes in terms of my relationships with ministers and priests since my choice to work for the church. It has been a very large struggle. While at Bellarmine, I decided I wanted to devote more time to social justice issues, and so I left a very comfortable situation in which I was respected among other faculty members. It was a hard goodbye, but I really felt it was time to go on to larger things. Then I started to work with an ecumenical group that worked with hunger. It was an extremely painful job, and after six months we ran out of funds. The guy who was running it was a horrible administrator and had misused all the money. I got slapped in the face by reality very quickly when that happened. That's when I decided to complete my degree in administration with the hopes of working for the church.

That also turned out to be a painful process. I applied for archdiocesan jobs that were available in all kinds of areas, and was always considered but never got the jobs. It was interesting, because I knew it had nothing to do with my qualifications in terms of work background. It became clearer and clearer to me that I wasn't getting jobs because number one, I was a woman, and number two, I wasn't afraid to say what I wanted to say. I think many men—and this is especially true of priests—found me to be threatening when I went in for an interview. A couple of times I found myself asking whether or not I really wanted to work for the church and go through all of this. Something always kept bringing me back, saying there would be a place soon.

In one case, the priest kept calling it "some nun's job" or something like that, and it turned out to be a glorified secretary. I didn't want to perform that way, and I could just visualize the kind of woman that was going to get the job: a very nice, soft-spoken person. The first time I met here I was pissed, because she had exactly that image. I do have harsh feelings about people who are afraid to deal with women who speak frankly and intelligently. I've done some real soul-searching about that, about how I come across, and I think the Lord is saying to me that you have to be truthful and you have to be honest and you have to tell people about how you would react in a job situation. So I am comfortable with that; but I am sad because I feel that a lot of people in positions that are safe don't really challenge what needs to be challenged.

I have strong feelings about how the church welcomes people: I think it does a very poor job. We get to be comfortable in tight little circles and are not the kind of church that opens its arms and says, "Come in and help us. Let's grow together." Being a single person in the church struck me very strongly when I moved here to Seattle and went shopping for a parish. It was one of the most important processes I've ever gone through, coming new and having no one know me, wanting to feel part of it and not being made to feel welcome. The first day I came here, I was thinking what a neat place and how much I was going to like it. Then I made the necessary steps to go from that to being really a part of the community. There were a lot of steps to be taken. You know, first we all signed little pieces of paper saying how happy we'd be to be doing more things, and there just wasn't the response. Organizationally, nobody would follow through on the stuff. One night for some reason I had the priest over for dinner, and I said, "All right, do you want us to work in your parish or not?" So now I've become involved, but what became very clear to me in the process was that I knew I had to persevere and go out of my way in order to do so. I can't help thinking in the back of my mind of all the people who are afraid or not willing to do that and who are gone. That, to me, is very sad.

In college I ran around with a large group of people and did a lot of things and had a lot of fun, but I really felt a lack the whole time in terms of my sense of spirituality. Even the campus ministry team was not anywhere near where I was. They were into sitting down on Friday nights and planning liturgies, and I was into going to parties. I got into going to liturgies, but always feeling a loss because I wanted to do something else. I really felt that there wasn't any kind of reaching out to the whole group of people that I felt was a large majority.

So I ended up applying for the Jesuit Volunteer Corps. It was never important for me to want to make a lot of money. The way I wanted to live was in a simpler lifestyle, and I wanted to be a person concerned about justice. I don't think any of those ideas was clear in my mind at the time, but I was looking for a situation where I could do something of service. I think my reasons are much differ-ent now for being involved than they were then. I wanted to feel "needed by". I think it was much more personal than it was other. Maybe it's the difference between charity and justice.

I am not the kind of person who spends time talking about how God is a vital part of my life, and I am not really Bible centered. I would say that it is definitely Jesus who is the center, but I don't get into that "Jesus jargon." The question that is clear to me is, how can we live the way we live when other people are suffering? I've always been rather issue oriented, I guess. When it became clear to me somewhere along that line that we had to do something, then I think I went back to see what scripture was saying and saw that Jesus is the way. I began looking at the kind of people he was reaching out to, and it became clearer to me what we should be involved in. I don't think I have any alternative like going into subur-bia and living a nine-to-five lifestyle. It would be enough to make me puke. I couldn't handle it after all of my recent experiences.

I've built a whole different kind of community support group. I think there is a real danger, though, in that the temptation is there, once you do build community, to let it become exclusive. This would be fine, and yet I think there is a larger challenge. I am just finishing up with a five-year relationship with a man, so right now I am not into marriage. I think in many ways I am attracted to religious life, but in essence I don't think I want that. I find the support the most attractive part in that, but I also see it as running away from the challenge that we have to be involved in, which is to be able to say that it is all right to be a single laywoman in the church, that there is a place for us. I think more women who are thinking of religious life are also staying away from the bureaucracy and confinement of it. A lot of women are hired because they are sisters, and I know if I was one I would have a lot easier time of it in some ways, but I don't want to run away from the challenge of the laywoman in the church. It is important to be part of that struggle. I am definitely for women to be ordained, though at this time that is not a desire for myself. There are many women who are already ministers, but without the recognition. I don't think I am called to celibacy, and I don't think that is going to happen because of my goals in community living.

I moved into a community situation for financial reasons once. You meet all kinds of people in a situation like that. Some you become tolerant of, some you really live with, and some you just can't. There you have to learn to say yes and no. But I think that is the way I want to go. I want to be a woman who is respected and a woman who can provide leadership for the church. I want to be so totally into the justice stuff that I can explain it clearly to people so they understand what I am doing and why I am doing it.

LAURENE BRADY

(Pine Ridge, South Dakota.) Occupation: Math teacher at a college on a reservation.

Chief Calico owned the land where our convent, the Calico Convent, is located. I presently teach math in the junior college on the reservation. The Indian people started the junior college about five years ago, Indian controlled, Indian everything, but most of the teachers are still white. One of the chief aims of the college is to get people prepared to take over our jobs.

Our reservation is a rectangle, one hundred miles by fifty miles. The college consists of nine trailers scattered around the reservation, and we go to the trailers to teach the people in each district. We are connected with Black Hills State College, but there are problems with that. For instance, it is required that to teach for college credit, you have to have a master's in the area you are teaching. Well, who has a master's in Lakota culture or language? Our aim is to get people prepared academically so they can go out and teach without those problems.

I've been here six years now. I like the lifestyle very much, and I definitely see a need to be here. I like the open air and the earthiness of the people around and where we live, and I like the freedom of leaving our doors open to everyone. I am not in a large group now, and it is easy to live this kind of open lifestyle. We have a trailer. Young kids feel free to come in and take a bath and spend the night, because a lot of them don't have indoor plumbing. The teenagers come and say, "Can we use your shower?" and then they'll stay and watch TV and spend the night on the floor, or in a spare bed if we happen to have one. Or people can feel free to just come and visit and stay for a meal. Whatever we have we'll give them, and they know that.

Before Pine Ridge, I was nine years in Wichita, Kansas, at a large boarding school for the rich. Then I went and got my master's at Notre Dame and returned to elite Wichita. I was principal for three years at a parish school. After that I taught math for a few years, and then went to Pine Ridge.

I had always felt bad about our convents because they were too enclosed. I wanted challenge in academic teaching, so I wrote to a

lot of Indian schools and ended up here. I had never been to Pine
Ridge before. I needed enough money to move off the mission so
I could afford to live in this trailer. That's why I started to teach
college. I really found this necessary in order to be with the people.
We have a neat community, with the Marist brothers here too. We
share a lot of things: Eucharist, prayers, things, cars, money . . . a
really supportive group. There are five brothers, and then they have
lots of foster kids coming in and out.

When Indians move to the city, they often come back. This is
their home, where their roots are. Alcoholism has to be the biggest
problem on the reservation; there is no doubt about that. The problem is with both males and females, but it is the woman who definitely holds the family together. The grandmothers are beautiful.
They take over the little children, and they are not young. Amelia,
for instance, is in her seventies, and she has ten grandchildren.
They are from all her different families. She is a beautiful lady. They
all live off the land, and they never rush. What the heck, what are
you going to rush for?

We were just talking about that. I was working in our infirmary at
the motherhouse and everybody was going crazy. As soon as mass
was over, everybody rushes. We take all the wheelchairs, rush them
back to the infirmary, and then sit there all day waiting. I certainly
felt it more this time returning to the motherhouse than six years
ago. Everybody got their baths by 10:30, and we had the rest of the
day. Now, the Indians would just say we really live stupidly.

We live in a very different culture. If someone comes and asks for
a sleeping bag, we hesitate to give it because we may never see it
again. The Indians ask for them all the time because they are sleeping out all the time. Okay, we've lost more sleeping bags. The last
time, a girl asked for two sleeping bags, and they were hanging right
up there, so I couldn't say no, yet I knew we would never see those
bags again. The same girl had forty dollars taken from her, and her
response was that someone else needed it more than she did. She
doesn't have any money, but that's the disposition of those pec ˈle:
if someone has a greater need, then that thing doesn't belong to you
anymore.

They have beautiful spiritual customs. Their spiritual life does rub
off on you. Forty percent might even say they are Catholic if it
came to filling out a hospital form, but that doesn't mean they are
practicing. They have beautiful peace pipe ceremonies, beautiful
healing ceremonies. They still practice the old, traditional way, bring-

ing their little altars and herbs and setting them right in the middle.
That's why the whole Catholicism thing leaves me with real
questions.

I feel that I am here because there is a need to be here, but that
is true anywhere—even the expensive homes of Wichita. I just particularly feel there is a need to be in the open somewhere and with
this kind of people right now. I think I am receiving more than I am
bringing anything. I have really learned so much from them. Personally, there is no way I am here to give them my spirituality, because
theirs is far more spirit oriented than mine will ever be. The Indians
have a very earthy spirituality. Our Sioux have certain rites that cor-
respond very beautifully with our Christian sacraments. For example, they have what is called "oblation," where they go out into a
sweat box to get purified, and then they go out to the mountains
alone for about four or five days waiting for a vision, fasting, praying
. . . waiting for a message from God. And they have healing ceremonies. This girl . . . I don't know what happened to her. I think
someone slipped her some dope or something, because she was
hallucinating. It lasted four days. They had a medicine man who
came with his little packet of sage and herbs and his peace pipe.
The whole room was in total darkness. The windows were covered
with blankets, and for several hours they prayed for her. Then
everybody smoked the peace pipe all the way around, even the par-
ticipants. Sometimes they don't let the whites participate, but they
offered it to us to smoke. There is a ritual in how you hold it, and it
is very sacredly done.

Afterwards, you always eat stew and fry bread. Everybody brings
their own bowl and spoon, and a big pot of stew is passed around,
and the fry bread, and cake and coffee. They have beautiful give-
aways, too. You know how you bring presents to someone? Well,
they would give it away. For example, if someone dies, the day of
the funeral they will have a big dinner afterwards and then they give
away all the person's possessions. They will also give away anything
that they have that is sacred to them. They may have been making
quilts all year long, and they give certain people these quilts. I think
they save things from giveaway to giveaway, like we do.

Certainly in my own life, creation has taken on a whole new
meaning. The earth has got to be a much more sacred place for me
now than it was six years ago. I find it very difficult to go to a cute
little retreat house. Once I was in this huge room that was just ele-
gant in Colorado Springs, and it bothered me. It wouldn't have six

years ago, but now I have a whole different creative aspect, a different concept of God's creation and what it can do for people.

One of the problems I could get into very easily is to get too provincial at Pine Ridge when there is a whole world out there. I think the same thing is true of male-female relationships. They have to be there to make you whole, to make you more of a person, to make you more filled. But I think a lot of turning it off has just been patterned or programmed into our lives as religious. If you didn't know a different way of life—if you entered the convent at the age of sixteen and got programmed into your head that male-female relationships could be bad and lead to all kinds of bad things—what else would you know? You were confined to the four walls of the convent, and the priest came for mass, and you served him in the priests' dining room—well, it's built right into the program. I don't think it was healthy. I certainly am a much freer person now, and I also enjoy the support of our intercommunity. We are not worried about what we look like when we see each other and so on. The male certainly has something to bring to us. They are the ones who are the good cooks, and they are the ones who wash the dishes. There is really no stereotyping of roles in our community.

Sexuality is part of spirituality. It all comes back to being a fuller human person, as far as I am concerned. The more fully human you are, the more you can give. I guess my spirituality is based on the concept, "Act justly, love tenderly, and walk humbly with your God." The earthly things and the Indian way of life and my intercommunity make me better able to do all of that. And this means every person, including the drunk man who might come to the door, whom you might fear to let in because you don't really know what he is going to do. There is a little tenseness there, but I think it makes me a richer person.

CHAPTER FIVE:
BEING OPPRESSED

"I think men need to understand what it means to be violated, to have your private person violated, before they can understand how women feel about rape, about being touched, about being looked up as an object. I go down to the beach a lot, and I have to walk through a park. There are a lot of guys hanging out there. I can't just walk through the park as a human being, you know, I'm an object to be commented upon."

——Jackie Berry, Hawaii

JACKIE BERRY "That's my downfall: I analyze the hell out of everything and that's a real barrier to spirituality. There are feelings inside me too."

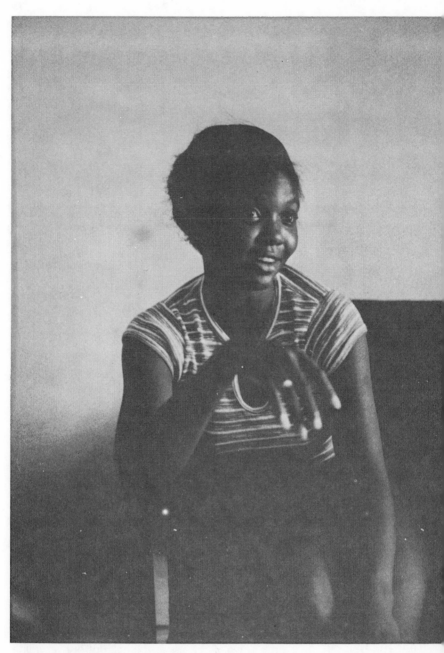

PRIVATE EDNA HARRIS "The men don't have to do the same things as women in the same job. We are not treated fairly at all."

MARY FLOY GREEN "I wanted Buddhism in America."

MARY GARRICK "My first communion was the happiest day of my life."

JACKIE BERRY "It doesn't seem like I belong anywhere."

JACKIE BERRY *(Honolulu, Hawaii.) Education: M.A. in political science.*

Divorced.

I'm told you can have very good friendships with men, but I've never experienced it. Without sex, male friendships aren't too deep. There is always a sexual tension with every man at some point. When I was young, sex was the thing you used to get a man. I grew up in the fifties, with a strange kind of morality, and I'm still caught in it. I was pregnant when I married Doc, and that's why we got married. For a long time I thought the only reason he married me was for sex. His life went on in all sorts of ways that didn't include me. He never seemed to pay any attention to me except in bed. I had his full attention there!

Now that we're divorced, I realize what a gift my husband was. He saw my faults and still loved me. I look upon his love as a gift to me, and I feel a lot of guilt. That's the problem in my relationship with Dick. Maybe this is always true in relationships, whether it's sexual, male-female relationships or any kind of relationship, female-female. Dick is so perfect. I don't mean he is a perfect person, he's got faults, but he's decided on a certain lifestyle he wants, and he's pretty perfect within those parameters. For him, not to have a drink is not a sacrifice. Other priorities in his life weed out those wasted energies. That part of him is very threatening for me, because it might take him away from me. He is a searcher, and that doesn't allow for a commitment. He hasn't had a relationship since his marriage broke up in his early twenties. He's never lived with anyone. He's a real loner. He's had long-term relationships, but I'm the first woman he's ever even committed to living with.

I was raised in a family of five, but I have a different father from the others. My mother got pregnant with me when she was seventeen years old, and my biological father was killed before I was born. Then she married the man I call daddy, who was in the navy. I have one sister and three brothers. I also sort of lived with an aunt and uncle whom my mother was very close to. I got a neat family history when I was with my aunt. I think there were thirteen kids,

and she was the youngest. Her mother was sixty when she was
born. A sister who was twenty years her senior sort of raised her.

I have almost no childhood memories until first grade, and they
they are not very good. I hated my father. They told me when I was
sixteen that they had arrested my father, and all I can remember
thinking is, "What a relief," because I felt guilty that I hated him and
now I didn't have to feel guilty anymore. Now I like him; now I
understand him. But he used to beat me and my brother who is
below me because we were both sassy. I always had a point to
prove. He hit me so hard once that I couldn't hear for three days.
He was real worried. He is kind of a typical childbeater—you know,
not a mean man, but a man who is not in control of himself. I can
remember I would make him so mad that his face would go red and
puff up, and the only way he knew to release that was to hit.

Question: Did you fear your husband would do that?

Answer: Yes. Once in a while he used to tease me and say, "You
don't like to be cornered." He would get me in a corner and he
would put his arms out like that. I would go berserk and start crying. I guess that was the fear of the male, just knowing that they are
physically stronger.

I am not afraid of rape, but I am afraid of being physically hurt, of
someone hitting me. I guess I see men as a potential danger,
whereas I don't see women that way. Oh well, that's not true. I can
remember, it was in Reno. I was walking along and there was this
large woman—not real tall, but real muscular—and there was just
something about her that scared me. I don't know why. Women
aren't friendly to you. I mean, they don't start talking to you. They
smile at you sometimes; they sort of look at you and then go. I
think maybe I might be a threat to them. Here is a woman doing
something that is not acceptable to them. I think people are always
a little afraid of the unknown.

One time I went out to the north shore with some friends and
rented a beach house. I was jogging along the beach. I had done it
every day—this was my third day, I guess—and I was coming back.
I wasn't far from the house, and this young guy, a punk, probably
about fourteen or fifteen years old, was coming towards me. As he
got almost parallel to me, he dodged down and grabbed me at the
crotch. I turned around and called him. I said, "You little Fucker!
Come here and I'll twist that right off." I just wanted to go up to him
and grab his penis and have him feel what it feels like being violated.

I experience in knowing that males can do what I cannot do. For instance, recently I talked to Dick on the phone and he told me about this nice experience he had in Italy. When I got off the phone I went out for a walk, and I realized that I was actually mad, that there was a part of me that was angry, and I was trying to figure that out. That anger came from the fact that I couldn't do the same thing, that I have to use a lot of caution on a trip because I am a female. I don't feel safe hitchhiking or going camping. He could be robbed, I guess, but it's a different kind of fear. He could make plans without thinking of it. He could walk down the street to get a beer or buy a cup of coffee at ten at night and not have to think about what other people will think about him doing that, and he won't be cornered.

I was raised a Baptist: no smoking, no drinking, no dancing. The church told me not to do those things, but my parents weren't very religious and they did. So I was half and half. I think I was the only one in the family that got hooked on church; I really liked it. I was in love with Jesus. Good Friday services were cathartic. I would just cry my eyes out. How could such a beautiful person who loves everybody . . . ? My family wasn't that way at all. They thought I was a little weird.

I remember the night. I was about nineteen or twenty. I was living in Los Angeles with another girl. I went to bed and I started thinking about God, and I realized that there was a possibility that God didn't exist. It was an awful experience. It was traumatic. I remember looking out the window and trying to figure it out, looking at the stars and wondering why I felt that way and being real scared about something that had been very secure in my life. Religion had given me stability, so when I started questioning that it was very upsetting. Then I met Doc, and he was a Catholic who had fallen. He called himself an existentialist. For a long time I believed that there is no life after death, that there are no givens, and that everything is relative. I believe now that there is something. I think it is possibly true about reincarnation.

I read an article by Elisabeth Ku³bler-Ross, and she believes that there is a unit out there that we all come from. Arthur Koestler is another who believes in that same idea—that we die and our spirit goes somewhere. What happens once we get there, I don't know.

I had a neat experience in Ojai, California. A lot of people believe there is some kind of energy in the mountains there. A friend of mine took her son who has cystic fibrosis there. She was investigat-

ing other avenues of healing rather than our Western ones. She had
taken him to an acupuncturist, and now he is going to this woman
in Ojai who apparently has healing abilities. It was a beautiful place,
set in the middle of the mountains. There were about five people
about my age, and everybody else was fifty, sixty, seventy, or eighty
years old. We meditated and had a service. They mentioned Jesus
coming back, and we meditated for peace. They had a little United
Nations flag everywhere.

There was this marvelous little old lady. I would guess her age to
be somewhere around ninety. She was a fragile-looking person. She
had this pink dress on, pink slippers like Alice in Wonderland, and
little white socks, and white hair all piled up on her head and the
cutest-looking face. There was love and kindness in her face. She led
a little meditation exercise, and I remember her telling us to think
about love and peace and goodness. She embodied all those qualities. That's what I mean by spirituality.

It doesn't seem like I belong anywhere. I can't find a lifestyle or a
group of people that I feel totally comfortable with. I'd sure feel
better about myself if I could come to terms with some things. I
think what I am talking about is coming to terms with myself and
growing from there spiritually. How do you do that?

An example I could think of is when Linda and I were in Ojai. It
was very spiritually oriented, a feeding of the soul. I would jog every
day, and we would go to these interesting places and she would give
me some readings and we would talk about what they meant. The
only definition of spirituality I could give you for me is finding that
place within myself. I think in order to be a spiritual person you
have to have that peace within yourself, and then you can give of
yourself.

I needed a change, to get away for a while, so I made the decision
that I would leave Hawaii. I didn't have any expectations. I was
scared and very nervous about it. I didn't know if I would like it, I
just knew that whatever happened it would be a way for me to learn
more about myself. I realized how comfortable I had gotten in
Hawaii, and that maybe in order to grow more I needed to change
my physical state. I find that if I am comfortable, I don't grow. I just
enjoy, and that's okay, but I just needed to change.

I've never been alone in my life, and I'm not good at handling
being alone. I think it is valuable to learn to be alone without being
lonely. Part of this trip was for me to learn that. I find that I'm not
bored with myself when I'm doing something, but I get lonely when I

just sit. I get up in the morning and go out by the lake and have my coffee and walk. I need to be doing something. I couldn't just go sit in the woods, but I would go and walk for two hours in the woods. Sometimes my thoughts are just boring. I like being alone when I know that I am going to be meeting someone later.

I started on a backpacking climb with three women, and we climbed back into the mountains to a beautiful waterfall and found a neat pool. Going up the valley I at first felt a lot of fear within myself because we were alone and I was scared. Do you ever get that fear that is like a little black cloud, but disappears somewhere along the way and you don't have any idea why? We found this beautiful pool and took off all our clothes and went in, and it felt so good. We got up on the rock and there I was sunning myself like a giant toad. There was an incredible sense of peace, very quiet except for the insects and birds, and you could just hear the waterfall. I experienced a real sense of completeness, and I felt good about myself and didn't want to be anywhere else at the moment. I wasn't looking ahead or thinking back. I probably felt like a butterfly feels: it doesn't analyze things. That's my downfall: I analyze the hell out of everything, and that's a real barrier to spirituality. There are feelings inside me, too.

PRIVATE EDNA HARRIS

(Fort Benning, Georgia.) Occupation: Dental assistant; enlisted military personnel. Age: 22. Education: Some college.

Married; no children.

When I was born we lived in Maywood, Illinois, but I don't remember much of it at all because we moved around this area when I was very young. Then we moved to Alabama. I have six brothers and four sisters. Compared to some that was a medium-size family, but here at Fort Benning, that is large.

My husband was stationed in the Philippines when we got married. I was in high school then, so I came here to Georgia to finish school. Then my husband thought I should go to college, but I didn't really want to. I did take some quarters in junior college, but what I really wanted to do was join the army to be with him. I took the first test when I was seventeen, but my husband said no. Then I took the test again when I was nineteen, and he still said no, only stronger. Then when I was twenty-one, I just told him I was going to the army to enlist, so I did.

When I first started, they said I could go into personnel record keeping and then after about eighteen months there would be an opening in the dental school. My husband influenced me a lot in that choice; he's a hygienist. He used to talk about teeth all the time like they were little bitty people, and I got really hooked on it.

That personnel record-keeping job was really boring. I wasn't interested in typing in school. I never would take it, and everybody couldn't believe that a girl didn't know how to type. So when I couldn't pass the typing test, they were going to put me down for supply clerk. I said I didn't want to do that, I wanted to be a dental assistant, and they should put me down for what I wanted. So they put me down for dental assistant, but at the same time said they didn't think I'd make it. Well, I did. My husband came up every week from Fort Benning to see me while I was at Fort Sam training to be a dental assistant.

I was stationed here in Fort Benning to be with my husband. But

I didn't want to work with him. I thought that would be too much, and he agreed. I've known him for about thirteen years, and I still find him to be the most fantastic man I've ever met. We went together for five years. My mother would not let me date until I was seventeen years old. My birthday was in June, and we got married in November. I knew, no matter what anybody was telling me, this was the man I wanted. We haven't had any kids, with both of us going to school, but we plan to have children in a few years. You would be surprised how much you don't know about a person even though you've been living with him a long time. At least you need to give yourselves some time to get to know each other. He agreed with that. Lots of my friends that had kids right away are saying how tied down they are. I think that's part of the problem with some of their marriages: married so soon, at eighteen, and then tied down right away with three kids running around.

In my own childhood there were eleven of us kids, but my mother was beautiful. She didn't believe in whipping either. It was a life full of arguments, but we learned to share because of my mother. It was just plain crowded, and it was noisy. When we are at home, I mean, we are home. We are a late family; it's nothing for us to be up till one or two in the morning. It was hard to adjust after marrying. It was lonely. You'd be surprised. My appetite even changed. There just weren't very many people to share with.

Several of my brothers and sisters have graduated, and I have a brother in college right now. I notice my mother is a lot freer with the younger ones now than she was with us. They don't have to do half what we had to do at home. When I came home from school, everybody had something to do. Now my sister might come home and read, maybe take a nap. Before, there were no "girl jobs" and no "boy jobs." If the dishes were dirty and it was the boys that used them, then it was the boys that cleaned them. Now, when I go home, mother cooks and everybody eats and then leaves, with all the dishes left there. When we were at home, we wouldn't think of leaving the table without washing the dishes, and she wouldn't even have to tell us. Of course now dishwashing turns into a major war, but my mother is getting very tired now. She works all the time, and so does my father. Both of them are finding all that noise hard. She probably does the dishes because it's easier. My brothers and sisters don't particularly like it when I come home now because I tell them what they should be doing. Of course they give it back to me with "You all so perfect." We laugh a lot, have a good time.

My mother was everything to my family when I was growing. She was the spirit that gave us all life and real care for each other, and taught us what it was like to love and have a place we called home. My mama was everything.

I'm working because I want to. Some women work because they support their whole family, and there are some who just can't and are on welfare. When a mother bends over backwards to get what she or her boyfriend likes and then gets wieners for the kids, well, I don't think that's right. I can see why some women don't want to work, but you can't just cut out welfare because there are really people who just can't help themselves. That's what makes it so bad, when some people make this a racket. They are so good at making a racket out of welfare that the government won't even get to them. And while this is going on, there are people who really need it. Some people are really angry about welfare. They feel that you are taking money from them, and it's not just their money. You'd be surprised about how many people there are that don't want welfare but just can't get a job.

I don't really expect to get a good job when I get out of the service. If you're not certified, you don't get what a certified person gets. At first when I got married I thought I was going to be like my mother—you know, cook, clean house, wash. After a while, I found the more things you have, the more confusion there is. And the same for family: the more people you have to go see, the more houses you have to have dinner in, the more tiring it gets. My mother doesn't mind when I just come at any time, but I mind. I like people to be invited to my house. It's gotten so that on weekdays I just don't like to be bothered about visitors and housework.

If I had kids I think I would want to stay at home with them and not work. You find some people that say they will take care of your kids and have a kind of daycare service. But I personally have known people to take care of kids only for the money. Sometimes these people even take the lunch the kids bring and maybe give them a cracker, or give them a sandwich that was in the bag but not the fruit and milk that were in the bag. They do it out of greed, and maybe resentment for having to take care of someone else's kid. I would never have a child in a daycare center. When my mother started to go to work and my brother Reggie was only seven months old, I was really upset. Finally she said she would wait until Reggie could talk. I just didn't want my brother or my sister mistreated like that.

We stayed with my grandmother and my aunt sometimes. My
mother had to be at work at six o'clock, but if she had to get up
earlier to make us breakfast, she would do it. She would cook our
supper the night before and put it in the refrigerator. I can't even
remember a night I woke up and she wasn't there. So by the time
my grandmother came, she really didn't have that much to do. I had
one aunt that came to take care of us. My own mother had raised
one of her girls when she went to New York for a while. Well, when
she came she just watched television, and sometimes she didn't
even get us lunch. Her daughter stayed in the house with her, and
she'd lock the doors and not let us in. Then about ten minutes
before mama came home she'd unlock the doors. Well, for one
thing, we had to get water from the hydrant and were outside all
day, from early in the morning until five at night. When mama came
home she was mad when I told her. Why, she didn't even wash the
dishes, and my mom had cleaned up after her kid! I know my
grandmother thought the way she treated my mother was wrong.

In my own work with other women, I feel like I'm in some sort of
fashion show. It isn't only a matter of going to work, it is a matter of
outdoing the other. We wear uniforms. Even when they talk they
tease, trying to put the other down. It is very competitive, and I
don't like a whole lot of the women in the field because of it. It's too
hard to get close to the real person. They also give you the impression they don't need the work, they are just doing it.

Another thing is that the men don't have to do the same things as
women in the same job. Men don't have to clean the floor. Well,
those men went to the same school that I did, and they should have
this room clean just like I have to have it clean. Even the doctors
are prejudiced that way: they would rather have a woman assistant
because they don't expect the guys to do as much as we do. We
are not treated fairly at all. There are some things that are just not
expected of men, and that's not right, because they were taught the
same things we were.

I've got one man, and I'm glad for what I've got. I am committed
to him. To me, if you care about the man, and he cares about you,
then what you choose to do is all right. But if they don't really care,
then the next day one or the other is off with another partner and
there is abortion and so on. I think there is a standard people
should choose to live by regarding sex, and I think that that standard comes from the way you are taught. For me that was mostly
from my mother. But I'm twenty-two years old, and that doesn't

mean I have to do everything my husband tells me. I've got my own head. I don't think I have to go to bed anytime he wants to. My feelings about that are so strong. I feel if he really wants us to stay together, he will treat me with respect. When we started going with each other and he started asking me to sleep with him, I didn't feel he was ready to really get involved. If we had slept together every time he wanted to, we probably wouldn't have stayed together. He wasn't ready; he even says that now. For one thing, he was too young and I was too young. When we did, it was because it was something I wanted to do, and not because I wanted to keep him.

I'm Baptist, but I went to church because my mother told me to. I didn't even start appreciating church until a certain age, when I felt it was the right thing. But as a child, I just didn't want to go. A lot of times, in my teens, when we wanted to go out Sunday night, my mama hated it, but we put up such a fuss that she let us go if we went to church that morning. That meant starting to get all cleaned up Saturday night, including the house, and then church on Sunday. Once I asked her why we had to go to the church on Sunday, and she said, "You are going to do everything I want you to do before you get to do what you want to do."

Right now, I don't feel that going to church makes you a Christian. I think being a Christian is what you feel as values, and church isn't needed for that. It is fine for fellowship and everything, but those churches are packed to overflowing, and a lot of that is a fashion show. I don't have to go to prove I am a Christian; I don't even have to talk about it. I feel that if I am a Christian then I live like one, and that is enough.

MARY FLOY GREEN   *(Boulder, Colorado.) Occupation:
Writer; welfare recipient. Age: 32.
Education: B.F.A. in ceramics, Wis-
consin State University.*

"Taking Refuge" is the first vow. It means you are formally joined to
the order of the Buddhists, that you agree to study the Buddhist
texts, and that you agree that the Buddha is the Lord God of your
existence. You say, "I take refuge in the Buddha." It truthfully is an
ecstatic moment in the relationship. It does not lend itself to the
mass media, because it requires the direct experience of the person
at that moment with their life, their integrity, their convictions. You
can get addicted to it as a brainwashing, as an attempt to be a
superperson. It's a P. R. scheme, the same as in politics. They say
the world is far from the point of enlightenment, far from the point
of buddhahood and the idea of compassion, which means, I see the
suffering of the world and I am sorry for it. I want women to know
that this is what they are going to be faced with if they come here.

I joined Chogyam Trungpa, Rinpoche, in about 1970, after I graduated from college. I was forced to have a child alone, and I was
with Trungpa Rinpoche because the father of the child decided to
neglect his responsibility. The guru gave him his compliments and
his support to do so. The people in the community were told by
Rinpoche that I was to achieve buddhahood through being a mother,
and that meant that none of them was to give me any help or assist-
ance of any kind.

I went into retreat and found out that as a woman I was allowed
authority in relating to the child, and that was all. Many women love
that situation where they are totally manipulated. Consistently you
are giving in to the role of woman as trapper, snare. Your whole life
is built on conniving what you want out of somebody and being
more beautiful than somebody else. They love it! Then they can go
around answering questions like, "What are you doing at the
Naropa Institute?" "Well, I'm studying child education from a Buddhist point of view." These are American women. They like to get
money and attention.

I have a religious side; some people do. I wanted Buddhism in America. I wanted meditation, a softening of ego, less pressure. I wanted American men to be able to have a choice. A man doesn't have to be aggressive to be acceptable and to be successful. I wanted to be vitally involved in America because I love her; to bring an alternative form of consciousness, to provide an alternative answer. I thought this is what I was buying with Trungpa. I was in love with a guy that was into Buddhism, and he was in India. I was looking for more understanding of what he was into. I didn't feel it was wrong to live with a religious nature, to want to live alternatively, not having to be in the mainstream consciousness. I liked what I knew about the man I was in love with.

KAY WELLS   *(Fort Benning, Georgia.)*

*Married to an army captain; two natural and
two adopted children.*

Military life is not easy. I'm not fond of moving every year. I would
like to stay somewhere forever, but that's what our life is: a year or
two here, a year or two there. Our home is wherever we are at.
There is no permanence. We have to do it that way.

We are very open and very affectionate as parents, whereas my
parents were never able to show they really loved me, and I always
felt unwanted. They show love to the grandchildren more than they
did to me. I have one sister who is five years younger, and we are
very different personalities. She was the type that would sulk and
pout and get her own way, but I was a fiery-tempered girl. I said
everything. That might be why my parents found it difficult to love
me. I was very rebellious.

I think they were busy trying to give me everything they never
had. When my daddy got out of the service, he'd been trained as a
technician and got a job, and when his boss finally died he got the
business. He was always working hard, but I had whatever I wanted.
They did love my sister more, though now, after their trip out here
on the Fourth, I can see they really do love me and care about me.
I had just thought I was a failure and that I really didn't turn out the
way they wanted. But the past is the past, and all I can do now is
try. My parents wouldn't understand. They would never believe
what I have gone through because they have not shown me affec-
tion. I went to therapy for a long time because I couldn't believe
there wasn't something wrong with me since they couldn't love me.
It really wasn't that they didn't love me, they just didn't show it, so I
couldn't believe it.

My twins are adopted. My parents were petrified when I was
going to adopt them. I was pregnant and lost the child I was carrying. I had cancer, and after I lived through that they told me they
didn't think I would ever be able to have children. However, I have
had two natural children since then. When we went to adopt the
twins they weren't born yet. We were very lucky. All of our children
are great gifts to us; they have all been miracles. Two years later I

got pregnant with David, and all the doctors wanted to terminate it, but I wouldn't let them. With my first baby they told me I was going to die, but I didn't feel that way at all with David. I was determined because I wanted that child so badly. We were married two and a half years with the first pregnancy. I felt that God had a reason for everything. If I'm meant to be here, I will live.

I had cancer twelve years ago now, and there has been no recurrence. The kind of cancer I had was a rare kind—only about two hundred of that class were recorded throughout the world. Chemotherapy was the greatest physical danger; they were pretty sure it would cure me if I could live through it. Then I had Becky, and we lost another child, and then I had David. When I saw the crown of his head, I knew everything was going to be all right. I wouldn't have missed seeing that for anything in the world. I can't imagine anyone not wanting to. Bill went with us the last time. He was sorry he missed it. He kept saying he couldn't watch me suffer.

Bill and I knew each other for three years before we got married. I was only nineteen. My daddy thought we got married too soon, but just because we got married after three weeks' engagement it really wasn't too soon; we knew each other. My attitude is that this is really it. I don't consider divorce as possible for me. My sister had a bad marriage and was divorced, and I always thought if it had been me, my parents would never have accepted this.

Sometimes the relationship between Bill and me is very difficult. At times we have talked it out. We have kind of gotten away from communication lately, but we're starting to again. When we first went back into the service after the ten months and he was going back to Vietnam, it was very hard for me to believe that he really loved me if he was going back there. I was upset about that for a long time. I didn't feel I was very important because he was choosing to take chances with his life. Partly, I think it was that my husband was used to a lot of responsibility, and he didn't have that in the business world. He went back to Vietnam because he really felt that it was the place to stop it, that it would come into this country next. I guess that's very idealistic, but that is really the way he feels. I know when it comes right down to it that Bill loves us. But if they say, "Do this," or, "Go," then that's what he will do.

We were in Germany for three years. We've moved over to Germany twice. We were told it was wonderful to go, and I'm never going to listen to people again. The first year we were there he was gone all the time. He was in the field or getting ready to go to the field. I was there with the children, two of them asthmatic, and I wasn't used to the climate, so I was sick too. I had a very bad situation there with the wives. We just didn't hit it off at all, and that's the first time I had somebody that I just could not tolerate. She pretty much told me, "You will do such and such. . . . " I knew when I was told that I would not do it, and I was insubordinate then. You can ruin your husband's career that way. It's funny how bad it got. I had a cast from my ankle to my hip, couldn't drive, with three kids and pregnant with David, and she was telling me I must learn that my husband's duty is the most important thing to him and that he loves being in the field. I was upset. She was trying to tell me that I was ruining his career.

But it isn't that way out here. It's like that on the outside too, in the big corporations, just as in the military. When my husband worked outside, the corporate life put a lot of pressure on us because we don't drink. That hasn't happened here in the military.

I told the lieutenants' wives that if they were with corporations they would be asked to do the same thing for their husbands, and they resented that. They were only asked to take part in coffee klatches and luncheons and stuff. They started saying, "You will do this," and, "Help such and such," and "Be a Red Cross Volunteer," and when they started telling me—well, no one is going to tell me. Then they tell me, "Well, you *are* in the military," and I tell them, "*I am not in the military!* I didn't sign any dotted line." They told us, "You are either a plus or a minus for your husband," and so I said, "I guess I'm a minus."

KAREN ARNOLD

(Fort Benning, Georgia.) Occupation: Veterinarian; enlisted military personnel. Age: 26.

In wartime this place would probably be closed down. The only reason we are here is because we have a military dog installation to take care of.

I joined the military in 1975 and get out next month. Job opportunities were scarce, so I joined up. All females are required to have a high school diploma, whereas males aren't because they usually end up in the infantry. When I went through basic, all the women trained alone and all the men trained alone. Now it's co-ed training, and they live in the same barracks.

There is a lot of physical training, a lot of classes on combat, drilling, and an awful lot of detail doing all the dirty work. Basic training is just to get you in physical condition and get you used to taking orders. When I went through, you only had to run half a mile. Now females have to run a mile and jump a five-foot ditch that is filled with water—and you have to be able to do it in a certain amount of time. When you hear a command, you perform it or you go to the gas chamber. You have to go into this gashouse and remove your mask without killing yourself. The tear gas releases, and if you've ever been through tear gas, you won't ever want to go through it again. They said the purpose was discipline, but to me it was harrassment.

They tell you when you join that you are not forced to go. You have to realize that. I joined partly because I knew I'd have a steady job and a paycheck coming in, and for the experience. Plus, you get a lot of benefits out of it afterwards. I can go to school when I get out and they will help pay for it. Part of it is to serve my country too, I guess. If there were a war or something, I guess I'd go. Some join up with a guarantee to go oversees. You can go anywhere over there—Germany. I spent two years over there and saw every country in Europe but England. If you can manage it right, you can do just about anything. I think the opportunity for travel is a lot of the reason for joining up, and a lot of it is to find a husband. If I

wanted to get married I could have just gone out and hung around
bars and found somebody and gotten married, just like that. A lot of
girls get married while they are in the service, and a lot of marriages
break up while they are in service. I know a half-dozen people just
offhand that have been married and divorced several times. There
are a lot of people living together without being married. (That's
after they get out of basic.)

There are no homosexuals in the army, because you sign a
contract saying you are not a homosexual. There is a greater
increase of black guys now. They are trying to get out of the slum
areas, and a lot of them just come in to get money. Girls go out
with black men, and white guys resent it. The black guys are usually
the first ones to proposition you. They are the main ones that
bother me. I haven't met any I would trust to go out with. A lot
more females are going out with officers, but you rarely see a female
officer going out with an enlisted man. If I were in combat, I would
rather have a male in charge.

Mine is one of the accepted jobs in the army because it is very
close to being a nurse; it is just that it is for animals instead of
people. I really enjoy working with animals and seeing what's wrong
with them. This is one of the few jobs I was interested in, because
of the idea of healing these animals. Military people are notorious for
dumping animals. They get shipped out someplace and they can't
afford to take the dog, so they dump him. It's our responsibility to
either find homes for them or dispose of them, and most of the
animals are put to sleep.

I'm a Methodist. We used to go to church most of the time, but
our whole family just stopped going. We are all kind of religious, but
we don't feel any great need to go to church. I went once here, but
all I thought about was sleeping.

It seems to me that when I went to church, they kind of wanted
to control your whole way of thinking about God, about everything—almost like the army does, in a sense. Your whole life is supposed to be structured to one thing, one thought. They were very
rigid in the way they wanted you to behave, in what they wanted
you to do and not do. If it came down to a difference of opinion,
you looked to the Bible for the answer instead of trying to think by
common sense. It was too stifling. Religion is there on the side for
me, but it is not foremost in my thoughts. Before I take certain
actions, I'll think about it, but other than that it's there on the side. I
mean, I'll never lose it or anything, but I'm not going to let it take

over my life. It has tempered my language, though. It is so easy in the military to pick up filthy language.

My morality was mostly influenced by my parents. I don't think religion had so much to do with it. If I was going with somebody I probably still wouldn't go to bed with him until after we were married. That's something I was brought up with. I can accept it from somebody else; I am not going to condemn them for doing it, but I don't think I could. I would have to know somebody awfully well and know we were going to get married. To me, that was always something you waited for until after you were married. What some of my friends do is promiscuous. You know, going with guys and sleeping with them and stuff like that when you aren't married. I accept that from them, and they accept the fact that I don't. The more I see people running around, the more I want to wait. I think a guy who goes with somebody that's been sleeping around is not going to be sure of her.

I'm used to living in a house in the country woods with nobody around. So this drives me crazy—people all over all the time. It's like being in a military base, only you don't see anybody in a uniform. Where we are, there are only a couple of neighbors around us. We have woodland and everything else separating us. The city would be the last place I would live; I don't even want to visit there. I'll watch it in the movies, but I have no desire to go there. I would like to see the Statue of Liberty, the Empire State Building, the World Trade Center, but that's it. I am mostly in solitude here. If they put a roommate in with me, I would probably go crazy. We see hundreds of people every day, and I want to come home and be alone and just be able to think.

My room is the only place to go unless I drive out to the middle of nowhere. I don't ever go around here alone, especially at night. Women do not go around here alone. There are so many rapes, mostly infantry guys, and there have been a few murders on post. I can go outside the building because there is light out there, and I have one of those little protector spray things you squirt out, but you don't want to go walking around alone. You don't walk in any wooded areas alone or anything like that at night, because you never know what could be out there. At home, in Syracuse, New York, I can go out alone anytime but hunting season. I worry about getting shot because they go gun crazy then.

My favorite film this year was *Close Encounters*. My favorite books are sci-fi. I saw a flying saucer when I was a little kid. That film was very realistic; it was not sci-fi, it was science fact. If it hasn't already taken place, it will. We will be contacted. It was very refreshing to know there wasn't any killing in it, no violence, and no one got injured. All these years in sci-fi pictures, if somebody showed up from another world and they were a little different from us, they pulled out a gun. Like *Star Wars* was a space fantasy, a cowboy movie out in space.

CHRIS WEISS *(Hamlin, West Virginia.) Occupation: Potter.*

Divorced; remarried; a mother.

This is my second marriage. When I felt my first marriage was dis-integrating, I signed up for some courses in pottery. I had always liked to work with my hands, and I decided pottery was exactly what I wanted. I just really enjoyed it. I learned a lot, but I ran into some problems with the teacher, who didn't like women very much. That is not unusual; a lot of men potters think it's a macho thing, since big pots take a lot of strength. He would lose patience and be real judgmental about things I would do, because I enjoyed hand-building more and he was a wheel thrower.

Then I got divorced and married Bob. That was ten years ago. We moved to New York, and I had an open studio in my home. We lived there about four years, and I taught women mostly, and per-fected my skills, had shows and so on. When I qualified for a job at West Virginia State College, we bought this farm and moved out here. Life is fulfilling here in a way that is more of an inner thing. I'm very interested in people, but I work well by myself and without a lot of noise, and those two things I did not have in Long Island. I had lived in a big, shady house in suburbia and had a nice studio, but there were just too many people. I found myself responding to everything and everybody, and I would never get any work done. Whereas if I'm working by myself in my studio or thinking through what we are going to do with this camp or with the Women's Bur-eau things or whatever, I can concentrate my energy on that act of creativity. Many people find that it is very stimulating to have a lot of people around. That doesn't sound good to me at all, though I do miss the cultural advantages the city has to offer.

For me, my work is play. There really isn't a whole lot of differ-ence if you're happy with what you do all day long. I sometimes feel guilty because Bob is not yet doing what he likes full time. He really wants to be here on the farm with the kids, but he can't do that yet because we need the funds. I do end up feeling guilty when I've had a good day. If I've made a whole lot of pots or I've gone to a couple of meetings and talked with women and gotten all excited about this or that, I feel guilty because I'm enjoying this and I couldn't be doing what I am unless he was out doing a job. A lot of times I feel that I have to work harder at learning things or developing options for both of us so that at some point I can pull more of my share. But until all the kids get into school full time, there isn't very much I can do about it.

The difference between my first husband and my relationship with Bob now is the attitude my first husband had about owning regular control over my body, and that in marrying him I had given up certain rights. It was in small things, like I couldn't wear a nightgown to bed if he didn't want me to. He had certain needs that he thought were a man's rights. He needed sex × number of times a week, whereas if I didn't or if I did, that was immaterial. The difference primarily between Bob and him is that my relationship with my first husband started out sexually, but Bob was always my friend from the start, and then it developed into a sexual relationship. He is still my friend, and then we sleep together, not a whole lot because we are both pretty high-energy people during the day and we're tired at night. In a way, that's too bad, because you need to renew that energy if you're in a partnership.

In my first marriage I never had any kind of a climax. Sex was something that was done to me. Now it is something I participate in, and whether I have a climax or not really isn't important. It's the sharing. We do it together, and I always enjoy it. I never, never have felt in the ten years that we've been married, except maybe once or twice, that I had to have sex because that's what he needed. But that did happen a lot in my first marriage. Tensions would build up, and that was the way we got rid of them. Now if tension develops, I talk with him. I usually force the issue so that we can talk, because he never initiates it. The first year of our marriage we were doing that all the time because it was a really hard time. Sex is not used as a substitute for communicating in my second marriage.

I think as a dynamic between a couple, sex has generally been overrated by society, but as an expression of a personal relationship, sex is ultimately a part of it. When you really establish a close relationship with someone, you do want to have some sort of ultimate fulfillment, and so I can't imagine a relationship as deep as my husband's and mine not ending up at some point in bed. If you don't have that personal relationship with another person, be they male or female, then I think celibacy is an alternative. I don't think people need to have sex like you need food and drink, or sleep every night.

The most important thing that would connect a whole lot of these things is the act of creativity. It is a creative act to do something like what I did with the Women's Bureau, as it is to make a pot, as it is to start a camp, as it is to have a baby. I guess that the low points in my life are when I have been unable, through oppressive circumstances—because of personal problems, divorce, whatever—to be creative in any fashion. There were a lot of wasted years in my first marriage in terms of there not being a whole lot of things going on. I mean that quite literally. I was a caregiver in terms of supplying people's personal needs, and that was about it. There was nothing particularly coming from me because there was no process, so there was nothing going on.

I think the really effective way for changing society is small groups of people who concentrate in their own backyards. That became my philosophy at the time we were working for the civil rights movement. The blacks said thanks to us, but then added, "Go home and work in your own backyards." I took it to heart, and I have come to believe that for me, my backyard is where I feel most comfortable. You do what you can on your own, and you try to work with the community. If someone is interested in what you are doing, you do that with them. You make whatever skills you have available for other people's use.

My first husband was a university professor. I just couldn't do the faculty-cocktail wife bit, and I always sympathized with him because if that was the kind of wife he wanted it was just too bad we got married. One of the sources of difficulties between us was the whole question of how much witnessing (to use an old word) you do for whatever you feel—say about war, discrimination, and so on. At the time I was feeling very strongly about a number of issues, and I generally let people know by what I do. If they ask me, I tell them. Now, ever since Bob and I are married we've always agreed very much about our own commitments. We don't work on the same issues, but we basically have a commitment to things we think are important: pacifism, socialism, and so forth. In all our discussions and the changes that I've been through from, say, the early sixties through to the present, it seems clearer to me that there isn't just one answer for changing society but that people have to make decisions together about the way they run their lives. Bob has a Ph.D. in history, and he has always taught in colleges. He had already been fired from one place because of political activities, so when we decided to move here we also decided we were going to stay here and not jump around. My thing is pottery. I really like it. But he likes to teach. Unless it's the ideal atmosphere, he is not the sort of person that people are going to allow to teach the way he likes to teach, to teach the things he likes to teach, or to do the things he likes to do.

I was raised Episcopalian and went to church for many years before I became disillusioned with church generally. That primarily happened because of my commitment to social justice and the church's lack of it. I just could not reconcile the lifestyle of the priest or minister who had a great many material things and then went to minister to the poor and disadvantaged. I just can't do that. Bob was Jewish and left the faith for pretty much the same reason: materialism and a lack of commitment to social issues. What he saw was the synagogue's commitment to doors and windows and ceilings as opposed to ministry to the poor. When we worked together with the American Friends Service Committee, one of their requirements was that even though we were not Quakers we had meditation hour with the group. That was the way it began. As time went on we developed a way of meditation, plus we kept developing more times when that could be used as a way of solving some problems. It was a tremendously moving experience, and we definitely felt what the Quakers call the inner spirit among us. It affected us both, but more me than Bob, because Bob is committed to Judaism since he is a Jew. He would be left with Christianity if he were to try to develop a spirituality outside of that.

One of the things that has happened to me is that I seem to be spending a lot of time with younger women, thirty-five or so. Through the years I have come to feel really close to a lot of women; I am much more comfortable with women than with men. Part of this has to do with sexuality, in that women seem to be more accepting of me as a person both sexually and nonsexually. Men for the most part seem to want to interject some sort of male-female aspect into the relationship. It seems that women can form closer relationships with each other than men can with men or those between men and women, except for marriage. It must be partly that the whole male-female thing isn't there. A lot of times relationships with women will involve a lot of touching and sex—not sex in bed, but sex as a touching and feeling close. I mean, I feel very close physically sometimes to women in a way that I could never feel close with men except my husband.

MARY GARRICK   *(Tensed, Idaho.) Age: 84. Native American; daughter of an Indian chief.*

Married; raised husband's nieces and nephews.

Well, I came to this reservation in 1934, and I am eighty-four now. You know, the Indian woman is very intelligent, and her most important work is her extended family. They all go at their own pace and in their own way. Even in the classroom, the Indian never punishes a child. Of course, the young people when they are in their prime of youth start drinking, and the grandmother begins taking care of their children, and off they go to their drinking parties. But as soon as they become grandmothers, they stop just like that. They have what is called the "extended family," so the grandmother is really the Grand Mother. Most Indians are not alcoholic, but they drink to get rid of their problems. They have a right to be what they are. They are Indians and that is theirs by right.

Up to 1925, the Indians were never American citizens. I don't know how they could not be, because they were born here, but they were never accepted. When they were brought into American citizenship, they were given the right to have their own constitutions and courts and juries. The older people—that is, anyone over forty-nine—were running the reservations. If you were younger than that, you were a kid. Another thing was that they couldn't own their own land. Some was put aside for them, out of which the government took back a great deal. They are not under the jurisdiction of the state but of the federal government. They are doing all right. They have fine teachers, and the Indians are gradually taking over for themselves and keeping the Indian way.

I am too old to remember much about my childhood. I can just barely remember my old grandma. I was born here on this reservation. I've got five children left. My husband and I never had any children, but he had nieces and nephews, and I raised them since they were small. I was the only child in my family. I was an orphan. I was never taken to any celebration. My aunt was the one who raised me, and she was very strict. She had other children, but they died. In the wintertime I was raised in the sisters' school nearby the church. Oh, that was a good school. I was there when that building burned down, and that was way back. During the summertime, my old aunt would come and get me and then I'd be up in the mountains. I enjoyed that. Everything tasted good. We'd pick huckleberries mostly. We went with some of my aunt's friends and their kids, and once in a while a man came along. We never knew what movie pictures were. Nothing.

I remember the reservation because I grew up at the academy there. My old aunt was very religious, and I was brought up in the old-fashioned way. We went to church always, and she wouldn't let me go to the dances. I wished to go but I couldn't, and I accepted it. We were poor folk. We had to do some hustling. We put a garden out back, picked cherries and roots and all that Indian stuff.

I got married when I was nineteen. After that I never went out to work. I stayed home and put in a garden and raised chickens and pigs. My husband was a musician. He had an orchestra, the Garrick Orchestra. He could play any instrument. When he died, it went with him. He played all over—up towards Cooley Dam, Spokane, the peninsula, and even toward Montana. Once in a while I went with him, but I had kids to take care of and I could hardly get away. In those days you never had babysitters; I did the babysitting. I enjoyed myself, and I learned how to mix with white folks. That's why I have a lot of friends around here who are white.

I wanted children, but after I lost one I couldn't have anymore, so that's how I was able to take care of my husband's nieces and nephews. When their dad was dying he said to me, "I'm depending on you." They are all gone. I don't see them much now, but they come and check on me every now and then. The Seniors come and take care of me mostly, from Tensed. They clean my house and feed me.

I've had a decent life. My husband drank, though, and that was one of my big worries. When he was drinking I told him to stay away and not to come back, because I didn't want him to scare the kids. So he'd stay away until he was sober, and when he'd come back he'd get sick and hungover and all of that. I never thought of leaving him. When you are married by the church, I don't believe in separation. "Till death do us part," even if it hurts. That's my belief. And I've felt pretty bad at times.

My happiness is to go to church in the summer if I can. God is good, very good. Father Byrnes comes over every now and then to bring me communion, but he is getting old too. So when the weather gets bad I call someone to take me to church. That's one thing my husband believed in too. God is all over, and when I get so lonely I do some praying. My first communion was the happiest day of my life. I'll never forget that.

CHAPTER SIX:
TRANSCENDING
OUR CULTURE

"I pray a lot. I even give lessons on how to pray. I teach people how to see. I see a lot. I take people away to the farm and I teach them how to see. I play an awful lot. I have a lot of very good friends that play. We go out into the country and play. I have friends my age and we make believe. We are very dear friends. They call us 'the unholy trinity.' I think my greatest pleasure is being with my friends. My peaks have been when we really, truly communicate. When I find new things in people I know well, it always surprises me. Every time I think I've got them, it changes.

"Hardly anybody knows how to play. A lot of people make a hobby as much work as their work. Some people lie on the sand stiff as a board; they never feel the sand. They probably never took a magnifying glass and looked at all the different grains, and they don't see the ripples or the patterns in the sand. They never make believe they are a crab. I love to make believe. I think making believe is such fun."

——Mary Anderson, Oregon

"God has used me as an instrument for healing."
(Joan Sutherland)

MARY ANDERSON "It's okay to hurt together, too. With some people it's like bridging across, a friend that you bridge across with, constantly finding new depths and new places."

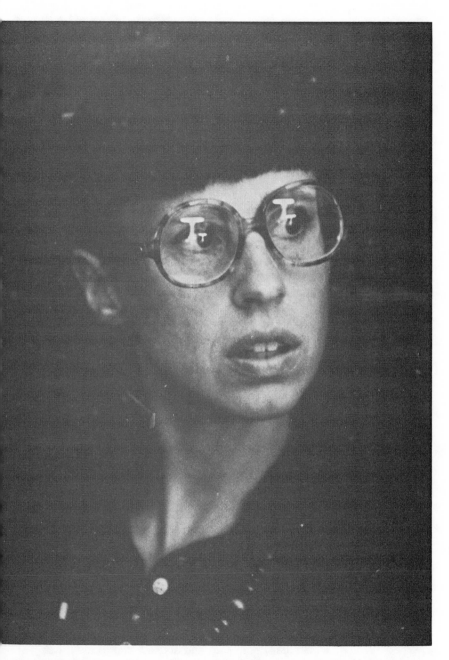

ELISE ROY "What I like to do most is engage in challenging relationships with all kinds of people in my life. Something mystical happens in a very short amount of time when I can so completely forget myself and enter into the other person. It's that touching-God experience."

MADELEINE SOPHIE GARY "Before I made my first holy communion, I
had already been sexually assaulted and abused, and to me it was just so
dumb, stupid person. The only thing that hurt me was that nobody cared

MARGARET DORGAN "We just don't have too much testimony of simple women, except perhaps in diaries."

JOAN SUTHERLAND *(West Virginia.) Occupation: Hermitess.*

The hardest thing was my first year in West Virginia. I had left everything, cut off all bridges, and found myself dumped in a little town of three hundred people in the mountains. I was working as a waitress. I was determined to stay one year, come hell or high water. I tried to live a basic contemplative life, but the pastor didn't understand. What bothered me was that I was not plugged in to the church. And I was out of the urban environment, away from cultural life. It was very provincial, and there was no one I could talk to. The closest place was a monastery three or four hours' drive away, and I couldn't be beating it over there every month.

One day when I was in my late twenties I was at prayer, and I heard a voice inside me say, "I want you to take the vow of virginity." I told the Lord, "You have got to be kidding." I didn't want to hear it, because it was death. I really fought it. Well, when I told him I'd at least give him a hearing, a real peace came over me, and that hung on for days. I guess that's the only real consolation I've known in my life, and I think from that the realization came that he was enough to fulfill me.

That was the beginning, the foot in the door. It has been a constant struggle, though. I have had to come to grips with who I am. My biggest fear was that I would not be fruitful, that I would never be whole. That it was death, not solitude. But this does not happen in solitude because that is where the deepest union and unification take place. Very deeply, we are really spouses of the Holy Spirit, and he is overshadowing us. The power of Jesus helps us in his word: "Abide in me and I in you, and you will bear much fruit." It is precisely because of the solitude that I can sustain the celibate relationship, because I am not sustaining it by the work that I do for God.

My fruits are fifty cans of green beans, twenty-five jars of fruit, and maybe a couple of pickles, but I don't have any fruits to look at. My fruitfulness has got to come in the Lord, and in the people who come to me for help. Well, maybe they do and maybe they don't.

No one human being could ever satisfy me. Only God could fulfill my heart, and I feel it is the same with married people. If I seek human consolation or human involvement for consolation, every-thing turns to ashes, but if God out of sheer generosity wants me to have human consolation, then it is a pure gift and it is real.

Talk about friendships. There are three priests with whom I have celibate friendships. I feel that in solitude you reach a communion with all other beings. When people come to me I regard their lives as holy ground not to be desecrated. Therefore I would not want genitality in relationships, because that is going to turn to ashes and I know it.

This touches on the mystery of death. The point for me is that my solitude makes me one with the Lord, and therefore I have fore-gone ties to the natural community. It is really a life agony wrestling with death, and so I could only do it as a celibate. If I am facing death, then part of celibate commitment is to die to union with others and also to die to the real desire to expand one's life by procreating.

I don't solve any problems for the people who come to me. If you can help carry a person's burdens, that is enough. They aren't your people. If nobody came, it really wouldn't matter. The essence is love, and it would work even if nobody came, if I took everybody into my heart and brought them to the Lord.

A hermit's life is lived beneath the level of forms. Part of this is cutting oneself off from society. We have a stereotyped notion of what a hermit is, someone out in the desert who can't get along with people. Sometimes hermits are confused with anchorites. They were walled in next to a church altar, and once in became station-ary. But the hermit had a great deal of freedom always, and gave hospitality. Freedom is an awesome willingness to be set in motion, willingness like that of the Israelites of old to move and respond. A real desert experience, because then you are surrendering to the Lord. You're not tied down to structures. You're alone, trying to listen to the spirit. You don't save anything for the next day. Merton said, "A hermit has to have a genuine call or else be thoroughly mad." A real vocation, a call to freedom and responsibility.

There is a story about a boy who was going to bed on a stormy night. He said his prayers and told his mother that he was scared. She replied, "God is going to be with you." He said, "I know, but I need a body with skin on it."

I need humanness. The hardest thing about celibacy is just facing yourself day after day: your quirks, listening to your emotions.

There are not a whole lot of diversions. The ultimate reality is that God is my father and he will provide me with all that I need. And he does this in a variety of ways.

For example, I don't have any money. The bishop gives me this place. I really, literally don't know where my next meal is coming from or whether I'll be able to pay the electric bill. I'm really not sure of anything on the material level. But if I can't find work and don't have any money, money will come to me when I need it. One of my priest friends calls them "love messages from the Lord." If I'm low on protein, someone might show up and give me a piece of meat. You have to live with me to see how it goes. For the past nine years I have never failed to meet a bill. God really takes care of me.

I remember once when we had no resident chaplain in town. I was snowed in and wanted a liturgy and the sacrament of reconciliation so bad I could taste it. So one Saturday morning I got a phone call from a priest friend. "How would you like a liturgy?" A perfect example of how God feeds me. He has given me certain people on my way who have met my needs. If I need someone to talk to, that comes in God's providential way. I just know, and that gives me courage. Once I had a cracked toilet seat and needed a broom, and someone showed up with those very items. I had a promise of work once but no job yet, and a priest arrived with two bags of groceries as if God had given him my shopping list. If I need something like curtains for the poustinia, curtains come in. That's just the way it is. It's God's show, and he can run it any way he wants. I don't think these things happen by coincidence. If you let God play God, he plays God. These are love messages from the Lord.

Some of the people who come to me I have a commitment to, to give them spiritual direction, and we have a heavy correspondence. Some come once a year on a long-term basis. Some come once, and that's all. Some are referred by a priest. Many more people are coming through now than five years ago. November to March I used to be assured of some solitude, but now there is more traffic. It is inevitable that people will come. People look for solitude in this day and age.

Two priests come once a month. Then there are the married couples. It's all part of a ministry of healing. I get a lot of women— West Virginia women, seminarians, religious—young and middle-aged people mostly. Some are referred by the abbot of a monastery in Wisconsin who is interested in the solitary life. Two sisters came who are interested in a more contemplative lifestyle. They were called to deep prayer and needed someone to say, "You're on the right track. You need two hours of prayer a day," or, "Read this." Local people also come: a lady whose mother is dying, those having marriage difficulties, people who have had a conversion experience, those in need of healing.

To me there is a direct correlation between how much I am hollowed out when I go before the Lord and how much he can fill them. I give them a cup of coffee, really listen to them, find space in my heart, pray to the Holy Spirit for his presence. And somehow what the Holy Spirit wants to get done will get done. I have seen this happen. The big thing for people is that you want to listen to them and pray with them—and something bigger: compassion.

That leads me to something else. God's light shines in our hearts when we're going too quickly or get disturbed. True purity of heart leads to compassion because we carry around our own burden. We do not sit in righteous judgment. We can give compassion because we can sense their struggle. If we have fought with our own chastity or our own anger—you know, we run the gamut; we don't have to be a saint—we don't sit in judgment. I can understand your struggle. What it is is mercy, God's mercy. I can take people into a hollowed-out heart and love them with no strings attached. One of the things we have to watch out for in the ministry is getting kicks from it. Hands off this holy ground.

A lot of men consider women good for sex and bearing children and for work. Some will refer to their wives as "my woman," "my heifer," or "my old lady." So I reflect back for them; I live alone, I am a woman, I don't have a husband, and I am making it. Women have told me this gives them courage. When a woman comes and tells me her husband is beating her, I tell her, "You don't have to take it; you can make it alone." They can see that I make it. It is part of celibate witness.

How am I affirmed as a woman in this culture? I am affirmed because I can work. My friends affirm me as a woman. Father Paul affirmed and encouraged me; and Father Cyprian told me, "You're not in this for yourself." I have brought into my solitude all the women of West Virginia, and somehow or other this is a holy struggle. The pain I have had to take—it's my redemptive suffering. I am not called to social action but to stay in my solitude and take the shit they give me, and somehow try to love them. It's a holy struggle, for all the women.

God has used me as an instrument for healing. For instance, I

became involved in a counseling relationship with a man that developed into affectionate ties. Should I cut this relationship off, or work
through it? I realized I had to consecrate the relationship to the
Lord and work through it. It was precisely as a woman that I did for
him what he needed, filled his need for greater intimacy. My celibate
commitment has helped others to work through the same thing
because I have had to work through it, too.

Women have come to me with all sorts of problems. One who
had a drunken husband came for shelter because she feared for her
life. Some have to ask permission to go away for a day to come see
me. I met a woman whose husband asks for sex every time he gets
drunk, and not only does she give it to him, but she kneels down
and prays for him before they go to bed. The role of women here is
conditioned by churches, but the real strength of West Virginia is in
her women. They are enduring and strong.

I can do this for women: reflect back to them, pray with them,
give them forgiveness and healing. I can listen, hold their hands, let
them cry, teach them to start becoming adults. I accept the lot—
take their husbands and forgive them. I want to carry burdens for
people, preach the gospel, teach them forgiveness and justice but
not to bow to unreasonable expectations. The good that happens
cancels out any of the pain and junk that I have to put up with.

MARY ANDERSON *(Portland, Oregon.) Occupation: Nurse; activist in Center for Urban Education (Cue).*

Married; mother of eight.

In solitude you're supposed to be alone, right? When I go down to the farm, I usually have a house full of people. I bring everybody else down there. I give them solitude by getting them to look in the same direction I'm looking. I discover it with them. I've tried solitude by going off and retreating by myself, but I always go to sleep. Stillness is something else; it could be really loud on the outside and you could be still on the inside. I guess it's a matter of focus. You could experience stillness even at a protest. I can think of a terribly still moment when there were thousands of people around, the ERA rally.

There could be twenty-five kids in the room talking and laughing and singing and playing games, and yet there is an inner stillness going on at the same time. You can just sense the contentment in the middle of lots of people. I have some pictures of it: the room is full of people, and a bunch of kids are over there playing games while the adults are sitting around here—some over there by the fireplace talking; some over there playing a game, rolling across each others' bodies; some over here on the couch together; somebody else in the kitchen, clearing the table. All these different activities going on in this one area, and there is a calm stillness in the house. All kinds of little relationships happening.

If there is one attribute of God that I would say is the most appealing to me it is the oneness, that God is one. I think that all has to be one, so when I see oneness happening between people, that feels like God to me. When I really communicate with a friend, really reach across, that has to be God. I can see it happening from my window here when I look in the park and see a father throwing his baby in the air, an old couple walking in the rain holding hands and looking up at the trees. The trees are full of the wind, and there are seagulls flying around, and the wind is blowing through the tree, and the couple is walking around the tree holding hands. There is a song about it: "Everything is part of everything anyway." That's community: coming into unity, being open to each other, people coming in and out and back and forth, an act of give and take.

I find the concept of institution very limiting. The institutional church per se does not allow you to be an adult. Name the attributes that the church has, and they are all parental attributes. The authority of the church, the teaching role of the church, the responsibility of the church for your spiritual welfare. I never knew Jesus before, never had any idea of who he was. I knew about the trinitarian concept of salvific expression and I knew about the ontological significance of the Trinity, but I never knew how Jesus loves and how he heals and how little he asks. You never even have to lift a finger; you're just loved. If you pour love into your children, all they can give is what has been given, all they can do is return. Maybe that is why our community has accomplished so much; because so much has been given to us, and so we have a lot to return. All the kids are falling in love and getting married; everybody is coming together. And everybody gives.

I've been waiting for a revolution for twenty-five years, but I don't know if I have the energy for a revolution. It would have to get a lot worse than it is. People have to be up against the wall before they revolt.

I think there is a legitimate call to celibacy, but I do not see why the vocation to priesthood or to religious life should be tied to celibacy. I personally can't see any value in it at all. I'm sorry about that.

When I think of what the church could be if you thought of authorship rather than authority! If the church was the author of the spiritual life, the people, then we really would have a viable church. I wonder if a pastor of a church parish has to be an ordained minister?

The spirit of the law and the letter of the law are two different things, and I think that human need should have a much higher priority than the letter of the law. When people are suffering from the effects of laws, then laws should be manipulated to end the suffering. I don't believe in divorce, but the idea we had in the old days about consummation has to be rethought. We were only thinking about physical consummation, but the physical is only one aspect of humanity. We also have our mental aspect, our psyche. How many people really achieve mental or emotional consummation just because their bodies unite? That doesn't mean unity. Maybe people should have to be married thirty-five years and then go before a tribunal and declare they are now consummated, physically, emotionally, and spiritually, now bound for ever and ever, amen. But until that time, it's kind of like taking final vows after years of living with.

I think too many of us are hiding ourselves from each other. My goodness, how we hide! Yet we are all the same; we all have the same needs and hopes and dreams. We're all going to be one someday. It's okay to hurt together, too. With some people it's like bridging across, a friend that you bridge across with, constantly finding new depths and new places. You don't have to know a person long. I think that is God, what happens between you and another person. That's Goding. God is a verb. A Unitarian minister once said in a dialogue, "God is what happens when love takes place." And I would hope always to pass that on to my children. The only thing I really try to pass on is that they should never look at life for what they can get out of it, but only for what they can put into it, because nothing else makes sense. All of nature blooms to give. There is no purpose of creation to take from life.

Things have to get bad before they can get better. You don't even know you've got an appendix to pop until it really hurts. Then you go get something done about it. You have to hurt before you really do anything about it. I used to read spiritual literature, you know, and I used to pray all the time. Then I got into theology, and I forgot how to pray. The more time we spend being consciously aware of God, the less we are really sensing what is going on about us.

I don't think anybody can make anybody else happy. I know people who try so hard to communicate, to come together and understand their feelings, and they do all this "in-depth communication" but never really get to know each other at all. I used to look at other marriages and think they were ideal and perfect, and ours was sort of . . . easy-going. It seems that all the people who worked and struggled and tried, who went to classes and marriage encounters, are the ones who broke up. I think people are too serious; I don't think you have to work that hard. My husband and I are incompatible: we have nothing in common other than that we know we are going to grow old together. We completely trust each other. He is an honest and good man and would never betray me, and he knows he has complete trust in me. Trust. So we are completely free. I can go anywhere I want to and do anything I want to. I am a sort of auxiliary to the radical movement, a bishopess. He does have a couple of really good lines that let me know he doesn't approve of all of the things that I do, but he respects what I do.

I'm a nurse, so my interest is really in health care. There was none available here, so we started our own medical clinic because of the needs we found. I'm a good starter, and I have lots of ideas to get things going. I gave birth to my clinic and then I helped found Cue. A friend and I were sitting in the backyard talking about it, and I feel now like I helped give birth to Cue there. The clinic has never been painful; we had so much support and encouragement and help with volunteers. It just grew and grew and grew, and finally we expelled it. With Cue, I am an urban monitor who watches the city and does investigations of trends and new developments, new problems. Then we go back to Cue and prepare training and education to equip us to respond to what's happening and what's changing and what's growing—anything that affects the viability of life.

I think that maybe the reason people in my generation got divorced when the first little crisis came along was because they married so that they could have a relationship with somebody else. As soon as you mature, you find yourself reaching out to others and wanting to cement a tie to somebody else and be loved. Now I think there are very beautiful relationships between people outside of marriage. You don't need a marriage license in order to find a real relationship.

I've lived long enough in the church to realize that the church changes so much and that the rules of the church are only rules. God is something else, thank goodness. As long as the church makes moral decisions, then for me there is no morality involved. If I am just obeying somebody else's demands, then I am disobedient; when I make decisions on my own, I become moral. I think the church has to look at us the way I look at my children. I put a lot of rules and regulations on them when they are young, and I give them a little bit of freedom here and there. Then the way they respond to that little bit of freedom lets me know how much more freedom I can give them. By the time they are adults, I want them to be able to make all of their decisions by themselves. We don't have an adult relationship with the church. I take into consideration the teachings of the church, but in making decisions on my own, I think along the lines of scientific thought and pragmatic practicalities. We have to know as much as there is to know about everything: the body, sexuality, and relating. Then we can make moral decisions and have responsibility for creation. There is a big difference between being an obedient person and being a moral person. To me conscience tells you values, and responding to and knowing your conscience is in you, not outside of you.

In my work here in the community clinic in the inner city—and I have five daughters and work with young people all the time—I don't see a lot of sexual promiscuity. Just to go a little further, what I do see and feel is a lot more freedom in relating to each other, a lot more responsibility in relationships. Sex has become a part of communication, a means of expressing something that is very deep. I see people, especially young people, relating so much more profoundly than we ever did when I was young. I was born too soon; I mean, we could not relate to each other. We couldn't get too close to somebody; you couldn't even embrace people. That's sad, terribly sad. Now that sex is accepted, we can go beyond that to the person, and there is not the fear. Now I am totally free to love anybody I find to love. I have a lot of male friends that I respect and admire, communicate with well, just because today there's not that sexual barrier between us. We kid around about our openness in communications. I don't think there is nearly the amount of sex there used to be when it was hidden. Bob and I are bound in marriage, so we do not have sexual freedom, but because other people are freed it seems to loosen everybody up.

ELISE ROY (Waterville, Maine.) Occupation: Artist, mystic, former x-ray technician. Education: High school.

Married; three children.

The value of solitude for me is in collecting myself. I've been dealing with a Christ identity that has kept recurring the last few years, and silence gives me time to do that.

I was an x-ray technician until I became pregnant. Now I have three children, and probably one of my most creative experiences was giving birth. That's such a high I can't put it into words. I am a Eucharistic minister, and I minister to the aged and dying. My work is to bring love and hope to the people I encounter, and that is my creative expression.

I am rather apolitical. Money doesn't really mean anything to me, though I know that sounds childish to say. My husband is an orthopedic surgeon, and I spend very little on myself. I practically dress out of the thrift shop. I make my own pants. I still spend a lot of money, but it's all on other people, on my old people. I don't even know how much comes in; I just spend what I need.

Jogging is very sensual. It is my greatest athletic thrill, even watching people run. I haven't encountered anything physical that takes on all of the things I'm trying to express the way jogging does. Sometimes its better than sex. I mean, it can really be euphoric. I can do things with my body that I never thought I could do. All of a sudden it's even changed my children's image of me. Mom's now Wonder Woman.

In my leisure time, I draw and write poetry, but that becomes discipline. What I like to do most is engage in challenging relationships with all kinds of people in my life. Something mystical happens in a very short amount of time when I can so completely forget myself and enter into the other person. It's that touching-God experience. Something happens about getting inside a whole lot of things, and there just aren't a lot of words to describe it. It's coming from inside of me, and it's kind of meditative.

Sometimes this happens when I am talking on the phone—in fact, the more intimate relationships happen on the phone, especially with priests, who will never tell me things face to face. I have a tremendous correspondence, too; I have a lot of intimate friends. My relationships with men and women both are very free. I don't get caught up in the sex difference, and I'm not afraid of physical expression. I approach each new relationship sexually, whether with a male or a female. I don't think any one man or woman fits the ideal person totally, but I do admire Pierre Teilhard de Chardin and Mother Teresa of Calcutta.

I'm not afraid of depression because I have an artistic temperament and I don't fight it. I get depressed when I've really worked hard at something and need to sort of gear down, so I cry or I talk it out. The right person almost always comes along. It isn't always my husband, because he's almost never there, and it's not my parents. I guess you would say it's almost always a friend.

I believe in celibacy as perhaps tied up with artistic expression. I wish I had a chance to try that. Yet there were stretches in my own marriage where because my husband was so tired we were kind of celibate for three weeks to a month, which I think is very long in a marriage. I wouldn't do this voluntarily, because basically I am a very horny person. It was just out of my control.

My husband and I are opposites. I don't know what drew us together, and sometimes I don't even know what keeps us together other than the fact that I need him. He complements me. I don't know if that is mutuality. We don't do a lot of things together, and I'm pretty independent. It takes a certain amount of tension in life to be or do anything creative. I suppose that if my marriage were such that I could not create, could not draw or write poetry, then I would choose divorce.

I had an affair once, but it wasn't very meaningful because we didn't have anything going intellectually. I can think now of a lot of men that I have very uninhibited relationships with. I don't sleep with them, of course, yet there is a sort of symbolic physical expression. And there is much more to it than the physical: it has a deep psychological or spiritual level to it too. I don't mean to degrade spirituality, but there is one man in particular that I can think of who is an atheist, and yet in our relationship I know he is the one closer to God. When I see him, I have to show him who I am with him and with God. All my relationships have that intensity about them.

With my husband, though, I have primarily a sexual relationship. In a way I'm kind of like Zelda Fitzgerald. He doesn't write about me, but he observes me, and I really give his life some pizzazz. It doesn't make any difference to me whether he looks at me that way or not. We do have a good relationship sexually, and he knows that's the thing that keeps us together, because he doesn't have the time or the interest or the energy to keep up with me. He gives me so much freedom because he trusts me. I've only been unfaithful to him once, and his response was so tremendous that from that time on I knew this was the man God wanted me to spend the rest of my life with. He was so forgiving. He didn't ask me any questions, or probe. It was more of a confession than any confession I've ever had. My husband is the kind of man who encompasses the sin I have committed and the forgiveness. And yet that's not everything. It's got to be the thousand other men and women I have to share my soul with. I've just got to share my soul with a lot of people.

I think one of my greatest inner resources is my spontaneity with discretion. I say "with discretion" because you can't just say what comes into your head all the time without also risking being cruel. Another valuable inner strength for me is my ability to touch somebody and not be afraid. The paradox in our society is that we are so touchy it doesn't mean a thing, but it really does mean something when I touch you. This kind of touching is like the laying on of hands; it is really going to heal you.

I've had religious experiences that are comparable to an orgasm. Being a Eucharistic minister is the greatest thing that has happened to me in my life. I was assigned some old people to tend to, and that is just the greatest thing. If anything happens unjustly to one of my old people, I get very angry. There is one beatitude: "Blessed are the pure of heart, for they shall see God." It's an experience in which you sort of transcend yourself—not just transcend, but become in communion with something greater than yourself. Prayer is not something worded, it is this thing that happens. Spirituality is something that transcends and encompasses everything you are, not just what happens in church or what happens when you are alone praying. It is what happens when I am with you, so that we really feel Christ between us.

A Poem
Giving birth is walking through the garden of God,
And He comes and says, "Here, take My flower."
And you reach up,
Near death,
And just barely touch God.

ANGELA MARTINEZ

(Albuquerque, New Mexico.) Age: 66. Education: "Not much."

Married; mother of sixteen children.

I was born in Mexico, but I grew up in Madrid, close to Santa Fe. There were just two in my family, me and my brother. When my mother passed away I was only nine, and then I stayed with my grandma. My grandma died when I was eleven or twelve, and my uncle brought me over here to the United States. My dad remarried, so I decided to come live with my uncle and his wife. They had five children. Then I got married when I was fifteen. That is the worst mistake to make. I never, never let my daughters get married so young. It's too hard on the woman: the job, the family, the husband.

I lived over in Madrid thirteen or fourteen years. It was a coal mining town, and it's a ghost town today. My husband was a miner. I gave birth to sixteen children; I have eleven girls. In 1932 there was a big explosion in the mines, and my uncle passed away in that explosion. Fourteen men were killed down in that mine. I decided we had to get away from the mines, so we moved to Albuquerque.

My husband became a truck driver here. My children slept in bunk beds, and they started helping out right away. The older children helped take care of the younger ones. I don't work now like I used to—it's too hard to move with arthritis in my legs—but when I was working I got up at four. I let the cereal cook while the kids got up and got dressed. I cleaned the kitchen, the floors, started the wash, started supper. I worked until eleven or twelve at night when I had to iron. I can't do that anymore. I am sixty-six, and my arthritis is so bad. I can't sit down, can't do anything. I don't like the TV programs, all the violence and killing, so when I can't sleep I get up and crochet.

Growing up was hard for me. For ten years my husband was away from the family. He went away to get work and then I was left with the family, trying to find work myself. It was just too hard to find work here. My son helped me so much while my husband was working in California.

The only thing that makes you happy is your sons. The only thing that's valuable in your marriage is your family. The hardest thing in my life was when my oldest died. He was very good for me, because he was special. He did so much for me. He was killed in a car accident. The oldest and the youngest ones were killed. First Junior; then three years later, Jamie. Jamie was good too, but he was younger, and I had all those other children by then. There are fourteen of my children left. I have lost two sons. My children are the value of my marriage. I give my life to them. I want to.

Most of my children have gone to college. They were encouraged to. They had to do the job they were given around the house, and then they had certain study hours, and they had to go to the library. When they were old enough they had to find a job and save the money to go to college. Even the girls did that. My brother loaned money for one of my girls to go to college, and then she paid him back. Some of my children won scholarships to college. Now all of the girls are married, and some are working. One went to nursing school and is on the faculty of the College of Nursing, and one had a scholarship to law school. She is raising a family, too, and has a little girl. I worked at five in the morning to help pay for clothes and books. My husband was plastering at that time. It was a real struggle.

My one daughter calls me long distance and cries. I start laughing, you know. I tell her to stop crying. I tell her she only has six children, and she just has to push a button for everything. When I came over here you had to pump the water. We had to wash one at a time, in a bowl. I had to do it all by myself—pump all the water and wash everything. Five I had in three years. Then the others, I had one every year.

MADELEINE SOPHIE GARY   *(Los Angeles, California.)*
Occupation: writer.

The basic thing that you have to do to "get over" to where you are
going is to follow the Ten Commandments. If you follow the basic
rules, then you don't have any real problems; it is simple. When I
was small, I hated being female—I swear before God I did—and I
tried my best to be a boy. You know, to do what the boys did to
show the people that I was worthy, because girls were just nothing.
Well, when I was about eight or ten, I found out that the reason
they were afraid of girls was because girls had babies. But nobody
would tell me where they got them from. All I knew was to keep
your legs crossed, pull your dress down and your drawers up, keep
a frown on your face, and pray. I did that, and I never got pregnant.

They always talk about how the Chinese and the Japanese bound
the girls' feet and threw them over the wall, but in our society we
had a behavior pattern and a social structure that kept the girls
bound. I remember getting sent home from school one day because
I jiggled. Thank God someone came home while I was trying to cut
them off so they wouldn't jiggle! I wanted to be accepted. I was the
only black at this school, and I spent years trying to get white. See
the scars I have here? The teacher told me I was never going to get
white, so I started to commit suicide. I wanted to get out of the
way. Then they locked me up. I thought being colored was some
kind of disease. Everything that went wrong, I was the culprit.

What I dislike about the women's lib movement is that they don't
have that intellectual wit you need. Wit is sharp; it gives you an
opportunity to escape oppression. That's what Roosevelt had. You
can do a lot of getting across. But they set up animosity. As far as
the women's movement goes, I've always been moving.

I have clairvoyance and ESP. Sometimes it is so sharp that I am
panic stricken, because the church doesn't believe in that stuff even
though they practice exorcism. Nothing is more weird than black
magic. In essence, it's exorcism, but yet if I say I have ESP or clairvoyance, then I have to say mea culpa, mea culpa. The thing of it
is, I knew I couldn't shake it, and when I can't shake it, I deal with
it. I made up my mind that whatever they said, God would give me

some witty answer. They sent me to a Jesuit psychiatrist. He was a wit, and we became friends.

When I get bored, honey, I sit there in that little room and plot things. You know, I ask the Lord the send me something to keep me balanced because so much has happened to me in my life and I've been through so much. Right now it's just an existence. I am really proud just to exist, because I believe that God has something he wants me to do. I'm still living. What I am trying to say is that most suicidal people forget that life is a gift, and regardless of how rough it gets, it is not yours to take. If you get a certain plateau where life has no meaning, and if you don't have something to fall back on to keep you living, you could just step over tomorrow. If you meet somebody that will let you rant and rave and scream and say all the wrong things, that is what helps you "get over." If they just let you pour this raw soul out, it's just around the corner, because God knows how much you can bear.

In some societies, women were once the boss. I think we have about three known women's primitive societies, all women. I can't go there, but if I could get ecclesiastical permission I would go, because each woman has seven husbands. It is somewhere along the Amazon. I am not arguing with the church because I feel like these men are going to excommunicate me. They already have excommunicated me from society. If you don't have a certain shape, a certain figure. . . . and my voice doesn't have that sweet delicacy to it. I am not the epitome of femininity.

I wanted to go in the convent where my mama worked. The reason was that even at a young age I knew what "first" meant. The first family. They are educated people, like the Kennedys. You know, what they call the elite, the blue book of America. Most of them went to the Convent of the Sacred Heart. I would go into their homes, and you could see the beauty. You could see the books. You could see people with their own rooms. You could see people with towels that matched, or were together in one piece. If you go into my bathroom and pick one up, you get this huge picture window in the middle of the washrag. You say to yourself, "Gee, how long can I psyche myself out?" I'm not poor; I'm affluent.

There are little tricks that I passed on to Stephen—Stephen Michael is the forty-fourth kid I raised—and I passed them on to the other children. When they were young, I took them around to the places I would go. I'd go to the door and say, "Good morning, madam. This is your friendly black person, and I am here because I would like to give my son or my daughter [whatever the case may be] or my children [there would be four or five of them] an intro-duction to what social living is." I always told the kids we were camping in, because we had orange crates and make-believe stuff. But I would like them to see how the other side camps in.

I was born in Chicago in the twenties. I was the youngest of about eight living children. There was a set of twins before me that died when my parents lived in rural Georgia. My mother went to work. We always lived in what you would call an upbeat community. We lived in Englewood when I was a child. The preface to my book *Jazzbow* is about my early childhood, till the age of seven. The reason I wrote it was to show people that if you have a will, not just the desire but the will, and are willing to work at it, then you can overcome regardless of what race you are. My platform is non-violence.

I live in a nice house. This house now has gone up on the market, and it's worth about $35,000. And you know, I don't eat but from one day to the next. I just go day by day, and I have all these oppressive problems.

I grew up in the era when girls couldn't play baseball and didn't drive cars. Girls didn't use hammers or nails or tacks. Well, I did, so everybody said I was queer. I grew up to hate the word "queer." I never felt that you had to put on lipstick and powder and paint to attract the opposite sex. I read somewhere in a book that that's why the baboon has a red rump, and when I went to the zoo and saw a baboon's behind, I swore I didn't want to wear lipstick. If I had to have all those outer things, I didn't want it. Before I made my first holy communion, I had already been sexually assaulted and abused, and to me it was just some dumb, stupid person. The only thing that hurt me was that nobody cared. You read in the paper when it happened to the white kids, but I couldn't tell anybody then, because if you did they always accused you of being on the other end.

It was that psychiatrist who really saved me, because he told me that I had a high IQ. I was twenty years ahead of my time, and I would have to pick my friends. He said it was difficult even for him to follow my phraseology. I gave a lecture at some psychiatric insti-tute once for a group of doctors, and they gave me a standing ova-tion for what I had to say. But when I left I was still just a nigger.

I spent most of my life escaping being anything but a person. I just didn't want to be fitted into stereotypes—female stereotypes,

gay stereotypes, black stereotypes. In my heart and in my mind and
in my whole existence, I am a being that God created, and therefore
in God's order of things I am somebody. I have to be somebody to
myself before I can be somebody to somebody else. It's too late for
me, but it's not too late for me to pass it on and help others who
have not had the experience and the extensive reading background.

In my childhood, even though people thought I was a happy kid, I
was totally unhappy. I felt not only child abuse, but I felt I was
abused because I was a girl. I didn't have any defense for it, and
then I tried to defend myself. You know, I learned how to fight karate.
It wasn't until last year that I found out I could have gone to a clinic
and changed my voice. I mean, my voice used to be even lower
than Tallulah Bankhead's, and that was a source of pain for me. I
always felt unloved and unwanted, and I had such unusual ideas.
Thank God I'm living today.

In 1956, I was fortunate enough to have a hysterectomy when I
didn't need it. Two weeks later they passed the law that they could
not remove any tissue from your body unless it was diseased, but it
was too late to help me. That was the turning point of my writing,
and of my life. Shortly after that, I began to go through all sorts of
traumatic changes, and nobody cared. The male doctors said, "It's
just a loss of a few parts," and nobody would listen. I had to suffer
in a religious context because I had been taught that to be a Christian is the worst thing that could have happened to me as a black
person. It's horrible if you are black, because religion keeps you
subjugated. It keeps you down; it keeps you oppressed; it keeps the
white man's foot on the black person's back. I am afraid to challenge even the priest for fear he is going to excommunicate me. I
have to make a choice, whether I follow my religion or not. I can't
follow my heart or my head and still be Catholic. The church lacks
soul as far as spirituality is concerned. But I read the story of St.
Martin de Tours, and I know sometimes the devil's busy running
around putting those obstacles in the way.

I'm writing a book called *Mastering the Leadership in Educational
Change*. It's going to be three volumes, for people who want to see
education change the negative polarization in the thinking of their
children that makes them captive to other people. You are enslaved
by this negative, so-called dogmatic teaching. It is so erroneous that
it affects you even in your secular life. My life has been service oriented. Now, at this late stage, I am trying to turn it around. I am
trying to learn how to live for me, and I don't know how. But

through living through others I feel I am doing God's will. That's why I want to put it in the book, so that millions can read it and see how I survived. Every single thing in this house except some of my books—but even most of them—has come out the trash. I've refurnished it and recycled it. All my life all I got was what nobody else wanted. Stephen Michael was the first exception. His mother said I always took the crippled and the maimed and the mentally retarded.

I have to write, because sometimes if I know I'm talking on the tape a different me comes. We used to laugh about it. Now you hear all about Eve and Sybil. My doctor tried to tell people Madaleine Sophie is not a depressive maniac; she is not this; she is not that. She has got all those people in there. I've got twenty-two books going at one time. There are a lot of people inside of me. I'm writing and I don't know what comes out. There is no way you could talk to me and get it all, for the simple reason that there is a little wheel going in my head. I control it, and when I get ready to say something to you, I know that it is being recorded, but I also know that I am intending to write about it or am in the process of writing about it. Most people tell me that as long as I am funny everybody loves me, but they don't want me to show an ounce of intellect. They don't want me if I'm intelligent.

My theory is that religion is a handicap. Catholicism is the worst religion in the world for any black to be a part of. It's no good. God is not male or female, but is everything. I am made in the image and likeness of God. My God is black and female. God is universal. The church is universal. There is no distinction. So you are wasting time if you worry about what sex or color God is, what some rule or regulation is. God is all merciful, all kind, and God doesn't send me disease to punish me. When I went to church I was unwanted, because you see my black face was the cause of the "white flight." And that with being poor.

MARGARET DORGAN *(Bucksport, Maine.) Occupation: Carmelite hermitess.*

I've been pondering daughters of our culture and what achievement was open to them. You see, women have had to interiorize their giftedness; they didn't really have an outlet. While men were planning their empires, women were home as colonials, but there was tremendous achievement in the spiritual order. They were able to take all that power which women have and make very significant spiritual achievements.

Julian of Norwich, even purely as a writer, ranks high in fourteenth-century literature. St. Theresa ranks high in Spanish literature. She's sixteenth-century, and it seems the Spanish language hadn't evolved much by then, whereas English at that time was way ahead. It started to emerge in the fourteenth century, so Julian was an emerging writer. By then England had begun to move out of Norman French, which had dominated the culture since the invasion by William the Conqueror. All the nobility spoke French, and often people who spoke English had so many different dialects that they couldn't understand each other.

Women at work haven't achieved much. We're being paid sixty percent of what a man gets for doing the same job. We're responding all the time to what is required of us as women, and it is very much dictated by the economic market. Right now women are absolutely necessary, just as child labor was a long time ago. We are necessary as low-paid workers. One-third of families depend on women's salaries. There will be no reverse of women as workers. We are in the force, but not drawing the same positions.

The family is under stress, with dual careers where the man and the woman are equally trying to achieve as career people. It is straining the relationship between male and female because there is no role model for this relationship and many men have been willing to have the parasitic wife. But I think that would be extremely dull, though it's nonthreatening to have a wife whose whole existence is in terms of me. Now, I'm thirty years out of Radcliffe, and it's something to see my classmates: their achievement is in terms of their husbands.

Simple women have left nothing, no testimony, except perhaps in diaries. So what do we do with that? Undoubtedly there was the supreme achievement of women who responded to what was demanded of them as role models. Don't forget, the energy of the woman of the past was so completely taken up physically after ten children. She was about ready to simply die. Her mental energies were completely absorbed in this, too. There are a few examples of women who wrote: Harriet Beecher Stowe, some women like that, but very few. Some thought of no achievement for their own daughters. For instance, Shakespeare's daughters were illiterate, and no achievement is recorded for them. Women find significance where they are told to find significance. Undoubtedly these women saw themselves as achieving. I think the farm woman is an example of this kind of woman: they feel their lives are significant. And you see this in nuns. What is a nun except a "producer," a producer carrying out the great plans of the almighty male ecclesiastical hierarchy. Yet nuns were always close to the people, and the man at the desk never was.

After years and years of silence, which was my choice, I'm not that used to expressing ideas and so on. More and more contemplative nuns are moving into speaking as representatives now. I was asked to teach a course, so I decided it was a great opportunity to make known to women what other women had achieved on the spiritual level. Just to give them a taste of three women, all of them quite different. Julian was an English woman; Theresa was Spanish; and Thérèse of Lisieux was a French girl from the nineteenth century. I wanted to show how each of them was very much a part of her century and transcended the limitations of her century. You can look at every one of them and see strong limitations, and at the same time you can see tremendous achievement. Every one of them is a teacher. Julian was an anchoress, which was very acceptable in her culture. She simply stayed there praying, but she was very available to the people because they came to an anchoress for counsel. These women are very interesting examples of spiritual geniuses who took hold of the matter of their own time and were able to transform it into high sanctity—into tremendous fulfillment. At the same time, you have to watch that interplay with the masculine forces in their own lifetimes. You can't find that out with Julian, because all we have is her book of revelations. The only one I can think of is with that priest, and it seems to have been very good. The church that Julian was in was really a messier church, and we're moving into being a messy church again. Julian might feel more at home with our church than she ever would have with the church of the forties and fifties.

In the past, the only place for a woman was in her home, protected by her father until she was married and then by her husband until she died. She might have had some relationship to her older sons. The only other place for a woman was the cloister, which was much more flexible than the cloister we know now. There was no in between for a noblewoman; there was no place for her to go. Her achievement had to be strictly as a member of a family that was dominated by males, or in the cloister where she had more independence, where she was one among equals in religious life.

The value of contemplative life is timeless. I am just delighted with what this whole experience has been. I think we have too many contemplatives. Any kind of life that is only for a few is going to be hard to get an understanding of. It doesn't bother me a bit if people think it's a kooky life; it's my life. I know people who are married to men I couldn't think of seeing every morning or three times a day, yet this person is obviously happy with this kind of life. Nobody says to her, "How can you stand being married to Joe?" but that's what they come to me with. "How can you stand being dedicated to Christ in this particular way?" You can talk and talk, and they won't understand at all. Probably the people who can understand the most are those who have had an experience of prayer. They get a sense of how total that can be, how being totally absorbed in a prayer relationship with God is a complete life. But we are in a pragmatic kind of culture, a "doers" culture. Americans are all doers, still pioneers. It's right in our character: if there is a moon up there, we are going to walk on it.

We have a male-dominated economy and we need women there now, not achieving as males but coming with a different experience. Males have no nurturing experience: they never stayed with sick relatives, they never even brought up a dog, so they themselves have never nurtured. We see this in our culture, in our economic system. As women move into power, we have to watch that we don't have more males in power. We need a strong sense of the nurturing, not hardboiled women. Nobody wants the masculine type. People are upset when they see women achieving in terms of quantity. They want quality, and we can give it to them, those nurturing qualities. Men fear that, though, but women can invite them to that joy. It's a joy to nurture. The more highly educated man has thought this out. We've got to do it together.

Postscript

The second most often asked question about this book is: What did you learn from the interviews?

On the journey, I had a vision. As I stood on the ledge overlooking the Grand Canyon, I decided to take a photograph. When I looked through the lens, I noticed what appeared to be an image outlined in the foreground of the rocks. It was a two-faced image, one male and one female. I asked Peggy to look through the lens, but she couldn't see the image. At first it frightened me, but later I realized how beautiful it was for it was whole, holy, a holy image of man and woman as one.

Several weeks later, still on this journey, I heard a voice in the mountains of Montana. Loud and clear, the voice stated: "Foretold favors in misty harboured visions." The image was frightening, but the voice really got me. I just listened.

About a year or so after the journey, I had a dream and in it I saw the cover of this book. It was bright red with green and white flowers, standing tall in a breezy field. Each flower contained the face of one of these women and above the field of green and white flowers was a flashing title I could not comprehend. In bold, black letters the words SOCIOLOGY and MYSTICISM blinked on and off like a neon sign on the dark and empty streets of New York.

The vision, the voice, the dream are with me still. So, when I'm asked what did I learn from this project, I find it difficult to answer. I could say I learned what you have learned by reading these stories, but somehow I don't think that will be enough, because we don't know what we think we know.

The first most often question about this book is: Why did you do it? That, I can answer. I did it to learn. Here's hoping you learned what we learned, and more.

C.R.